Inanna Hyper-Luminal

✳

By V.S. Ferguson

INANNA HYPER-LUMINAL

By V.S. Ferguson

Designed by The Ferguson Company
Seattle, Washington

Thel Dar Publishing Company
Seattle, Washington
1996

INANNA HYPER-LUMINAL

Part I: View from the Void
Part II: The Land of the Ellipse

For information contact
Thel Dar Publishing Co.
10002 Aurora Ave. N., #3392
Seattle, Washington 98133-9334

Cover and book design by
Barb Ferguson and The Ferguson Company
Seattle, Washington

Printed by Malloy Lithographing, Inc.
Ann Arbor, Michigan

ISBN 0-9647276-3-3

✻

This book
is dedicated
to all those
who long
for freedom.

CONTENTS

ACKNOWLEDGMENTS

I would like to thank, first and foremost, all of the people who read *Inanna Returns*, and especially those of you who wrote me such wonderful letters. Your appreciation for the book has often brought tears to my eyes. Inanna touched you and you were kind enough to share that with me.

I would also like to thank the many people who came to my lectures. I learned so much from you; in many ways your insightful questions made this sequel, *Inanna Hyper-Luminal*, possible. To my delight, I discovered how many of you are "waking up" and having multidimensional experiences.

I wish to thank Zecharia Sitchin for his support of my first book. Without Mr. Sitchin's relentless pursuit of his convictions in translating the cuneiform tablets as he read them, undaunted by convention, I would never have had my adventure with the beautiful and irrepressible Inanna.

I would also like to thank my husband, Charles, for all of his help; Tracey Cooper, for structural support; Quentin, for getting his degree in Engineering Physics; Anne and Gary, for the Mexico link; Sharon and Gary, for introducing me to the Commander and the Lady of the Garnets; Angela, for being a brilliant angel; Noh-Ra Amrani, for the Enki connection; Debbi and her wonderful children, Nicole, Michael, and Justin, for remembering.

I would like to extend my gratitude once again to Tera Thomas—who helped in so many ways to bring the first book, *Inanna Returns*, to life. I also thank Barbara Marciniak for recommending it in her newsletter, *The Pleiadian Times*. I now fully realize how much courage both of these ladies have.

Thanks to Barb Ferguson for her terrific graphic design and consistently great customer service, and to Sara Lehman for her computer-osity.

I also would like to thank Pat Welch for her amazing brain; her intuitive ability to understand Inanna and friends, combined with her fervor for the editing process, are deeply appreciated by Inanna, Thel Dar, Gracie, etc. and me.

INTRODUCTION

Inanna Hyper-Luminal gives the reader the experience of being multidimensional. Our potential to access realities in various dimensions is latent within each and every one of us. When we began our adventure in the time/space continuum, we knew who we were. In this phase of the cycles of time, we have simply forgotten how to travel beyond the five senses. As this age draws to its inevitable conclusion and the veils are lifted, we will regain this endowment.

We are living in the Twilight of the Age of Conflict, or, as it is known in Sanskrit, the *Kali Yuga*. This is the final of four cycles which go to make up a day, a *Kalpa*, in the Mind of God. Because the veils of illusion in this cycle are at the ultimate depths of density, the Age of Conflict offers us the greatest opportunity to acquire life's real treasure—wisdom.

The first or golden age is the Age of Wisdom, the *Krita Yuga*. Prime Creator, in Its desire to experience Itself, separates Itself into numerous creator gods. All the gods begin to manifest their desired forms *knowing* they are equal parts of Prime Creator. In this age they express themselves freely, *knowing* and fully remembering who they are. The gods begin to project portions of themselves into the data-collecting vehicles they have created—meaning they incarnate into bodies to further experience their creation. They begin to feel a sense of loss and a longing for their original state.

In the second age, the Age of Ritual or *Treta Yuga*, the vibrational frequencies of the created Universe begin to diminish and the gods compete with each other for creative space. They desire power over each other and contemplate how to coerce the other gods to play *their* games.

They conceive rituals to bridge the potential un-formed world with the world of form. Initially, rituals allow the gods playing in form to access raw power from the un-formed, the Void. Although a weakened means of *focused conscious thought*, ritual becomes the intermediary mechanistic tool used to manipulate creative power from the "form" side of creation.

As the frequencies continue to *fall*, individual gods discover how to control the others. By exploiting the use of ritual, they trick the other gods into worshipping them, and thus generate an abundance of energy which they use to create all manner of fantastic illusory worlds. These clever gods build *immortal/spirit* bodies to inhabit the hierarchical worlds they create, and no longer incarnate in physical bodies, but rather enjoy the experiences of those who are incarnating.

In the third age, the Age of Doubt or the *Dvapara Yuga*, the frequencies of creation continue to increase in density. The gods in form begin to doubt; from doubt they lose memory, and forget who they are. They can still see the gods who are not in a third dimensional form and—in the course of forgetting—begin to worship them.

The wily gods who have ceased to incarnate continue to build illusory worlds, the Phantasmal Hierarchies of heavens and hells. While the gods in form become trapped in the cycles of reincarnation, they forget who they are and doubt the divinity within them.

The fourth age, the Age of Conflict or the *Kali Yuga*, is the period we have been living in since 3600 BC. The frequencies of time have further slowed, and the Visible World is surrounded by a dense web of somnolence. Our experience of time is altered; thus, the phantasmal worlds have become invisible to those of us living in this physical Newtonian realm. Today only a small number of people are able to see the so-called Invisible World; their ability to *see* has been inherited genetically because it was not bred out of their DNA. In other cycles such "sight" was our God-given right; but in the *Kali Yuga*, the veils are tightly drawn.

Because the gods have lost their capacity to *know* and to remember, writing—itself a symptom of the *Kali Yuga*—is established as the means of transmitting knowledge. There is no evidence of written history in the previous three cycles because it was not needed. What we do know is based on memorized oral transmissions inscribed during the *Kali Yuga*. Knowledge has been passed from generation to generation orally. Our command of memory today is a pathetic semblance in comparison. Only in the most ancient of texts, such as the Puranas, the Mahabharata, and certain Taoist and Tibetan writings, do we get a glimpse into the previous three cycles.

The Mahabharata and the Puranas contain lengthy predictions of what the *Kali Yuga* will be like, even fore-telling the availability of "fast food"—another symptom of this dark age.

In the Age of Conflict, the gods forget who they are and lose their innate ability to access their own inner divinity. Ironically, those tricky gods in their Phantasmal Hierarchies are just as trapped as those incarnating in the precarious and repetitive physical world—but they are pre-dictably reluctant to give up their power and to change.

In order to make way for the next cycle, a new Age of Wisdom, radiant-light Beings from outside this Universe enter to break up existing realities, and, in the final phases of the *Kali Yuga*, venture to assist all of the gods who long for their freedom. These Beings are gently guiding the birth of an enhanced data-collecting vehicle to be used by us in the coming golden age when we will again *remember* who we are.

Who wants to live forever in a created reality that has become stuck and frozen in a stagnant state?

As always, Prime Creator is moving on!

V.S. Ferguson, Seattle, 1996

CAST OF CHARACTERS

THEL DAR: A consciousness who dwells in the forever Void as hyper-luminal thought and displays itself as a radiant-light Being.

INANNA: One of Thel Dar's projections; the Goddess of Love from the artificial Pleiadian planet Nibiru and a member of the family of Anu.

GRACIE: One of Inanna's multidimensional selves who is living on planet Earth in the Twilight of the Kali Yuga.

OLNWYNN: Another of Inanna's multidimensional selves; the now deceased warrior king from ancient Ireland.

DIANA: Olynwynn's wife from ancient Ireland, and Gracie's current life mother.

BRENT: Olynwynn's brother from ancient Ireland, and Diana's recently deceased husband.

TATHATA: A hyper-luminal thought/radiant-light Being who also dwells in the forever Void, and is Thel Dar's friend.

JEHRAN: A projection of Tathata, and Inanna's Mr. Right.

WOLFIE: The famous composer Wolfgang Amadeus Mozart; a projection of Tathata.

CLARISSA: A new friend of Gracie's, and a multidimensional self of the Lady of the Garnets (wife of the Commander and Inanna's friend).

MICHAEL: Clarissa's true love, and a multidimensional self of the Commander.

ANU: Patriarch of the family of Anu; Inanna's great-grandfather.

ANTU: Anu's Pleiadian sister/wife.

ID: Anu's concubine, Princess of the Dragon People of Inner Earth; Enki's mother.

ENLIL: Son of Anu and Antu.

ENKI: Son of Anu and Id; genetic scientist.

NINHURSAG: A genetic scientist who is Anu's daughter by a renowned physician from Altair.

FILLED-WITH-STARS: Anu's multidimensional self.

MOONWATERS: Id's multidimensional self, and wife to Filled-with-Stars.

KEVALA, KARUNA, AND KHA: Three hyper-luminal thought/radiant-light Beings waiting for enhanced data-collecting vehicles.

I

DRIFT AWAY

Thel Dar lay poised silently in the vast darkness of the forever Void within the Mind of God. As a hyper-luminal consciousness, Thel Dar accessed the total panorama of nested layers in all-the-possible worlds throughout Infinity. No part of creation was too insignificant to observe lovingly.

In the Twilight of the Kali Yuga, Thel Dar had been working on an enhanced data-collector, a body/vehicle, through which fellow radiant-light Beings might express and experience Life. So when three Beings of a comfortable likeness to Thel Dar approached, appearing first as hyper-luminal thought and then as resplendent radiant-light Beings, Thel Dar knew why they had come.

"My dear friends," Thel Dar spoke, "I am doing my best. Soon there will be at least three sets of DNA enhanced sufficiently for your enjoyment."

The three, nodding in agreement, smiled with cheerful anticipation. Their question answered, they withdrew, leaving Thel Dar alone to complete the enhancement.

Curling up into the rich potent blackness, Thel Dar inhaled and focused on a location in the third dimension of planet Earth: the Pacific Northwest.

Clarissa, unable to lift her head from her pillow, stared at the white emptiness surrounding her. The once-cozy double bed now looked enormous, desolate. Michael had gone to Peru on a vision quest, and only the gods, whoever they were, knew when he might return to her. She felt abandoned and lonely; the bed was a mess and so was she.

She also felt ill. Doctors had told her there was nothing apparently wrong with her; all of her tests had come back clueless. Yet every day Clarissa felt a strange inexplicable "bubbling" inside of her. Confused and frightened, she wondered if her malaise had some connection to *The Wave* everyone was talking about, and lately she had begun to fear that she might not live to see the turn of the century.

The approaching end of the millennium had brought people to a frenzy; fearful of impending doom, they desperately sought answers. Some said this was the end of the Kali Yuga, the final stages of material illusion and spiritual darkness on the planet Earth. The coming new age would change everything. Feeling the change draw near, people attempted to adapt. Some clung ferociously to the past and their material possessions, while others abruptly left their homes and families to join cults or follow teachers. Others simply walked out into the desert to be alone with their God.

The Wave was understood to be an energy field in the form of an endless stream of photons—a sea of plasma coming from deep space, which invisibly emitted a high frequency of consciousness as it covered the Earth. It was said that those who chose to open themselves to *The Wave* would be assisted in adapting to the coming changes. *The Wave* would lift their cells into a higher vibration and activate the dormant DNA within them.

Reluctantly rising from her lonely bed, Clarissa decided to go for a walk. Perhaps the damp misty air would clear her head. The neighborhood she and Michael lived in was full of storybook houses. The tree-lined streets felt safe; this would be a perfect place to bring up children.

Clarissa desperately wanted to have Michael's children. They had met at the University and fallen in young love; Clarissa had never been with another man. She loved him with all her heart and, now that he was gone, felt as if half of her was missing.

Where was he right now? she asked herself, trying to imagine Machu Picchu or some coffee bar in Lima. Was he riding a rumbling mountain train, or drinking up smelly mushroom concoctions with a strange shaman? She hadn't told Michael that her cells were "bubbling." When would he come home?

A white picket fence caught Clarissa's eye. Behind it, thick plantings of snapdragons were bordered by rows of perfumed white alyssum and purple-blue lobelia, the kind that almost hurts your eyes with its beauty.

Clarissa stopped in her tracks, transfixed by the garden. There were old-fashioned roses, damask and moss, intoxicating perfumes; and herbs of every sort, basils, lavenders, and peppermints. Clarissa felt charmed by the garden's magic.

She looked up at the house and saw a woman sitting on the front porch feeding two large dogs little bites of cookies. The enormous dogs looked like wolves, but were grinning and wagging their tails.

"Hi there!" the woman called out.

"Hello. I was just admiring your garden. It's lovely."

"Come and have a cookie with us," invited the woman. "Don't worry, the dogs are friendly; they love everybody!"

Clarissa carefully assessed the happy demeanor of these beautiful creatures; she decided it was indeed safe to approach. (She herself preferred cats, but loved all animals.) Opening the white gate, she walked up to the house, which was beginning to feel oddly familiar.

"My name is Clarissa."

"I'm Gracie, and these sweet dogs are Bear and Rhiannon. Here, have a cookie. I was just about to make myself some coffee; will you join me?"

Clarissa nodded, smiling; as she shook Gracie's hand, she had the uncanny sense that somewhere, they had already met; somehow, they had always known each other. As Gracie headed for the kitchen, Clarissa heard the lyrics of a very old song coming from inside Gracie's house.

"...free my soul...and drift away."

Far away near the center of the Galaxy, Inanna, a beautiful blue lady from the Pleiadian planet Nibiru, stood in the Great Hall of the Intergalactic Federation Council waiting for an important conference to begin. The man she had long dreamed of meeting had just taken her hand in his.

"Allow me to introduce myself. My name is Jehran," he said softly. Inanna felt herself drawn into his eyes; and in the same moment, in the distant corridors of her mind, she heard sounds identifiable as Earth rock and roll.

"...free my soul...and drift away." Inanna scanned her consciousness and encountered Gracie, one of her multidimensional selves who lived on the planet Earth in the twentieth-century time-space continuum. These days, the impulse of Gracie's life force was coming across as a powerful frequency. Assuring herself after a moment that Gracie was all right and needed no immediate assistance, Inanna pulled her full awareness back into her present and allowed herself to melt into the fiery dark eyes of the man who had just introduced himself as Jehran.

Drifting into a kind of trance, Inanna thought of how long she had waited to meet her Mr. Right; and now here, at last, he stood before her. Her arduous journey into the erratic uncertainty of Earth's dense material realms had brought her face to face with Jehran.

Driven by her love for the human species, which had been genetically altered by her self-centered family, Inanna had projected herself into the race in a heroic attempt to activate the humans' latent DNA. Other members of her family—the family of Anu, her great-grandfather—had followed Inanna down into the vulnerability of flesh and blood. By inserting themselves throughout time, they hoped to restore the damaged human genome.

Around 500,000 Earth years ago, members of the family of Anu had colonized the Earth to extract gold for the depleted atmosphere of their own planet, Nibiru. Their chief scientists, Ninhursag and Enki, mutated the genes of a wild Earth creature, *Homo erectus*, with their Pleiadian genes, thus creating a race of slaves to work in the mines.

As the centuries passed, the complex power struggles

of the family of Anu continued to interfere with the natural evolution of the human race. The sons of Anu—Enlil and Enki—and their sons had quarreled endlessly, using Earth's inhabitants as combatants in pernicious family wars.

Enlil, Anu's favorite son, eventually resorted to using an awesome and terrible weapon, the great Gandiva. The ensuing massive destruction sent out waves of deadly radiation, alarming the entire Galaxy. The Intergalactic Federation Council then summoned the family of Anu to a conference, the agenda of which was to hold them accountable for their irresponsible actions. Restitution was demanded; a balancing was required. The Council decreed that the ability to evolve must be returned to the humans, and their DNA, which had been so artfully "unplugged," must be restored to its full capacities. Until this was accomplished, the entire family of Anu would find itself blocked by *The Wall*—prevented from evolving, and frozen in a state of boredom and stagnation.

This situation was further complicated by the reptilian tyrant Marduk. The intractable son of Enki, Marduk had refused to cooperate with the Council. He had already conquered the Earth and a good deal of the Pleiadian star system. Having no desire to evolve, Marduk had no intention of helping his family. He was perfectly content to remain in his elated state of tyranny over anyone and anything he could get his greedy claws on.

Inanna had taken the desperate first step of literally inserting a portion of herself into many multidimensional selves at different points throughout time. Fortunately, the adventure was beginning to show signs of success; one of Inanna's selves, the twentieth-century female named Gracie, appeared to be activating her latent DNA.

At long last, Inanna and her family had some good news to report to the Council. They hoped to convince the mysteriously powerful Etherians to remove the insidious invisible *Wall* which had made life so boring as of late.

Inanna was finding it difficult to remember anything as she let Jehran take her hand. *Jehran*...even his name sounded wonderful. Both floated in silence as they gazed into each other's eyes. For Inanna it was love at first sight, and from the look on his face, Jehran seemed to be feeling the very same way. The assembled crowds of various aliens, the Intergalactic Hall itself, even the stars above them all seemed to disappear. At long last, Inanna had met her equal.

II

FREE MY SOUL

A breathtaking piece of celestial music, a hymn to Prime Creator, announced the beginning of the Inter-Galactic Council meeting. Inanna knew she must join her great-grandfather Anu and the rest of her family. Reluctantly, she let go of Jehran's hand.

"I will find you after the meeting has concluded," he whispered to her. "You will have dinner with me?"

Inanna nodded, smiling, and hurried off; she was happy and excited, but she could not keep Anu and her grandfather, Enlil, waiting. She was looking forward to giving her report to the Council. Gracie's story would make Earth's future look brighter indeed. Inanna was proud that she had been able to assist the human race, which was beginning to evolve at last. But it proved impossible to keep Jehran's eyes and touch out of her thoughts. Inanna sighed deeply.

Anu stood up to address the Hall. He began by reporting on the condition of the Pleiadian star system and the readiness of his troops to facilitate their liberation from his grandson, Marduk. Anu and Enlil had formed alliances with all of the Pleiadian leaders who had been overthrown by the reptilian tyrant. These exiles were prepared to return to their rightful homes at the first indication that the majority of the human race had begun to evolve beyond tyranny, and was at last ready to join the rest of the Federation.

Olnwynn, one of Inanna's multidimensional selves, had accompanied her to the Intergalactic Hall. Being quite deceased as an Earth human, Olnwynn found it easy to attach his consciousness to Inanna's and to travel around with her. This warrior king from ancient Ireland was fascinated by the architecture of the Hall and the multitude of strange life forms from other worlds gathered there.

For instance, even though Olnwynn was a disembodied spirit, the Etherians could see him perfectly; but other beings walked right through him as though he wasn't there. He was getting used to such things, just as he had gotten used to being "dead," or at least to living outside a solid body. There had been many adjustments to make, including learning to time-travel, but he was very clever and adapted well.

He was certainly in a lot better shape than on the first day he found himself in Inanna's presence, with his throat slit from ear to ear. It had taken some time for him to accept the fact that he had behaved brutally back in the second century; had he been a better husband, perhaps his wife might not have taken his brother for her lover, and the two might not have conspired to have Olnwynn murdered by his own son.

As Anu began his speech to the Council, Olnwynn tried hard to listen attentively. He admired Anu, and sought to emulate this interstellar lord; like Olnwynn, Anu was an excellent leader, and very handsome too. But Olnwynn's thoughts drifted far from the great Hall in deep space to his lost life on Earth, back to his castle in ancient northern Ireland, to his pretty wife and his violent death. He missed his wife; he still loved her and wished there was something he could do to make amends for the terribly cruel way he had treated her. He no longer felt any anger toward her; after all, it was he who had driven her to murder, and he had now completely forgiven her. He did not seek revenge; he wanted forgiveness. He wanted to tell her that he still loved her and their son.

Olnwynn's dark green eyes began to twinkle. Both he and Gracie were among Inanna's multidimensional selves, and because he could easily project himself into Gracie's life, he often did so; it would be no problem to locate his wife, who was now living in the twentieth century as, ironically, Gracie's mother.

Inanna's multidimensional selves and their loved ones were frequently together, their lives amazingly interwoven throughout time. Gracie's mother, Diana, had married Brent, Olnwynn's brother from the second century. Brent and Diana had also borne a son who was the reincarnation of Diana and Olnwynn's son. Inanna had once explained to Olnwynn that the three—Diana, Brent, and their son— were bonded together by the murder they had committed. A powerful, ineluctable magnetism influenced the flow of life and the choices people made.

Olnwynn made up his mind to visit his wife in the

twentieth century, but he decided to stop by Gracie's new house first, to see how she and her black "wolves" were doing. Olnwynn loved the dogs, and he had grown very protective of Gracie.

Forming a tunnel of light by carefully imagining it in his mind, Olnwynn then threw his consciousness down the tunnel and landed on Gracie's front porch. There he found Gracie sitting happily with a new friend. The two were enjoying a hot drink which Olnwynn knew he had never tasted. He looked around for a beer or something else with alcohol in it, but there was only this new stuff which Gracie called "coffee." For a moment, Olnwynn wished that he still had all five glorious senses so he could taste the liquid in the girls' cups. But without a flesh-and-blood three-dimensional body, there wasn't much he could do but enjoy the memory of all the ales he had lustily consumed during his brief but zestful life.

Seeing that Gracie and her dogs were perfectly secure, Olnwynn moved on to the part of the country where Gracie had grown up, to pay a visit to his pretty, if somewhat ambitious, wife.

Diana stared blankly at her enormous luxury automobile. Brent had bought it for her just before the heart attack claimed him. Even though his temper had driven Diana to escape into a variety of tranquilizers and "mood elevators," she was lost now without Brent. Her entire life had centered around a man who controlled everything she did. She didn't know what to do without him; and now that she was alone, she found that she had no real friends.

Brent and Diana had been very wealthy and their social life had revolved around Brent's highly successful business. They had always been invited to society parties, and every Christmas they had received hundreds of greeting cards from business associates and employees. But in the two years since Brent's death, Diana learned that no one invited a lone widow anywhere, and the holidays now brought maybe half a dozen greeting cards. What had happened? Where were all those "friends" from the busy, festive times?

Diana ran her hand along the gold trim on her big car, then got inside. She wanted to go for a drive—anywhere, just to get out of the house. What was there left for her to do but go shopping? Her closets were full of unworn clothes; lately she had even stopped taking her purchases out of their boxes. Why bother? She never had anywhere to go, and no reason to wear any of them.

Last week, out for a drive like this, she had gotten lost trying to get home. She had lived in this same neighborhood all of her life. Why was her own home town beginning to appear strange and unfamiliar to her?

Olnwynn spotted Diana in her car and projected himself into the back seat; the front seat was already taken by Brent.

Brent was hanging around Diana because he too still loved her, and because he hadn't yet decided where to go since the fatal heart attack. He was busy telling Diana how and where to drive and lecturing her about spending too much money; but because Brent was physically dead and Diana didn't believe she could see or hear him, she didn't.

Brent turned angrily to Olnwynn and said, "What the hell are you doing here?" It took the two brothers a moment to recognize each other. Then, in response to his memories of Olnwynn, Brent began to shape-shift into the body he had occupied in second-century Ireland, as an entire lifetime played out in his mind.

"Hello, my brother!" Olnwynn greeted Brent. "By the gods, you're having difficulty holding onto a shape."

Brent shifted back into his twentieth-century body, even though his head was jammed with pictures from the past. He had envied his brother from the first day he heard tales of Olnwynn's bravery and skill in battle. Recalling how he had robbed his brother of castle, kingdom, and wife, Brent now felt a little uncomfortable facing his victim. When you're not occupying a physical body, there's no way to hide your thoughts or feelings. Death makes secrecy an anachronism; when you have nothing, you have nothing to hide.

As Brent was offering a weak apology, both men were suddenly thrown forward in the car. Diana's driving wasn't what it should be; she missed a stop sign, and slammed on her brakes to avoid hitting a large beer truck. Olnwynn saw a giant frosty glass of beer on the side of the truck, which made him very thirsty. Both men found themselves remembering the long evenings they had shared drinking and carousing together; there had been some good times, after all.

Diana was shaken. Narrowly averted accidents were becoming a common occurrence for her these days. She quickly pulled into a shopping area, parked her car, and stared blankly ahead. After a few moments, large red letters in a store window—"SALE!"—came into focus, and, comforted by this announcement, Diana got out of the car and went inside.

An ocean of furniture spread itself out in front of Diana. My goodness, she had never seen so much furniture. These new stores were all so big, how could you decide what you wanted? There was just too much to see.

Olnwynn and Brent hovered above Diana. Their love for this once beautiful, and now aging, *femme fatale* had brought them together again.

In the back of the store, a salesman was snoring away. The man, in his early sixties, had an earthy masculinity that gave him a knack for selling furniture to bored, lonely housewives. He was good at his job, but today he was sleeping off the beef enchiladas and three margaritas he had enjoyed at lunch.

Olnwynn saw his chance to temporarily take over the sleeping salesman's body. Once in, he stood up and walked toward Diana.

She was still lovely in a gracefully fading way. Her designer suit showed off her figure, which had always been amply endowed. She was quietly talking to herself: "What on earth am I doing in here? I have plenty of furniture."

The handsome furniture salesman approached her. "Madam, we are looking very beautiful today. What a fine woman you are!"

Diana blushed. She thought, *This man is so nice; well, so nice looking, anyway, so manly.* Diana missed having a "real" man around. The salesman told her to sit down and offered her a Coke. Diana loved it when men told her what to do; it reminded her of her Brent. Compliantly, she sat right down.

Diana looked into the stranger's eyes and saw a familiar light in them; love was flowing out of his eyes into her. The two talked for awhile about the weather, her children, good Mexican food; really, it didn't matter at all. Diana was feeling relaxed and somehow free; her hormones were once again flowing. The whole experience made her feel lighter, younger, and for the first time since Brent died, happy.

After awhile, Diana knew that she had to leave. Reluctantly she said good-bye to this kind, handsome man who had made her feel like a desirable woman again.

As Diana walked away, the bewildered furniture sales-man woke with a slight headache and tried to remember a conversation he had just dreamed. Or was it a dream? Had he been talking to the woman now leaving the store? *Naw,* he thought greedily, *she looks like serious money; I would have sold her the whole store.*

Olnwynn and Brent got back in the car with Diana, each in his own way feeling sad; they both loved this woman dearly. Feelings like jealousy and anger didn't seem so important now that they were out of their physical bod-ies. Whatever Brent and Diana had done to Olnwynn in a far and distant time didn't really matter in the big picture. Death was truly the great equalizer. Olnwynn forgave Brent and embraced the man who had once been his brother. He also made up his mind to make his way back to Diana again; this was just what Olnwynn needed to set himself free.

III

HER RED HAIR

Gracie returned to the front porch carrying a tray with fresh cookies and two steaming cups of coffee. She smiled at Clarissa as she recognized traces of heartache in the younger woman's eyes.

"Want to talk about it?" she asked.

Clarissa wasn't at all surprised that this stranger was able to read her present state of mind so accurately. She sensed that Gracie was the right person to tell her troubles to.

Tears streamed down Clarissa's pretty cheeks into her coffee cup. Gracie listened silently and patiently as Clarissa recalled how she and Michael had met at the University, and how she had known instinctively that Michael was the only man for her, that she would never love another. They had been happy together for several years.

Then Michael had been abducted by extraterrestrials. He disappeared for seven days, and when he came home, he told her that being with the extraterrestrials had been the most wonderful experience of his 28 years—the real beginning of his life. He told her that, of course, he had been frightened at first, but his new alien friends were loving and gentle. He was thrilled to be aboard their wonderful spaceship and to see firsthand their incredible technology. Michael forgot his fear and, for the first time in his entire life, he felt at *home*.

Michael explained that while he still loved Clarissa, there were things he had to do now, connections he must make, that took precedence over everything else in his life. A quantum change was coming to planet Earth. He and Clarissa were part of the change; but he had to be in Peru at Machu Picchu on the next full moon for the sunrise. And he had to go alone.

Michael promised her that he would come home to her, but he wasn't sure when that would be. And then he stuffed a few things into his backpack and left town.

Clarissa had cried herself to sleep for three days. It was all so confusing; first he had been missing and then he had gone away.

Clarissa and Michael had always believed in a higher good. They had talked about their shared beliefs, their hopes for a better world, a less violent future for the children they dreamed of having. They had meditated together and had shared an interest in various spiritual teachings, but this was different. Michael's abduction experience had radically transformed him, and Clarissa was afraid she had lost him.

Gracie smiled compassionately at her new friend. She knew very well that being in love can hurt.

"Clarissa," she said, "you must learn to trust and rely on yourself."

Clarissa looked up through her tears. "Trust *me*? How can I trust myself when I don't even know myself, who or what I am?"

"Do you ever meditate?" Gracie inquired.

"Yes, now and then." Clarissa was puzzled.

"Would you like to meditate with me?" Gracie's eyes twinkled. "I have a friend; perhaps she can help you. And maybe she can even tell you how and where your Michael is."

The two women stood up and walked into the house. Gracie's dogs followed, wagging their tails.

At last the meeting of the Intergalactic Council was over. Inanna had successfully presented her data and was busy looking around for her new friend, Jehran, when a very strong signal from one of her multidimensional selves came through. Gracie was calling Inanna from the planet Earth. Inanna had mastered the art of being in many times, places, and dimensions simultaneously. While still on the lookout for Jehran, Inanna projected a portion of her ever-increasing consciousness into a small living room in the Pacific Northwest.

Inanna appeared to Gracie and Clarissa as they sat silently in focused meditation. Clarissa was delighted to meet the beautiful blue lady, who, like Gracie, seemed strangely familiar to her.

"I am Inanna, Gracie's friend."

Clarissa, sighing deeply, asked sadly, "Can you tell me who has taken Michael, and if he is all right?"

Inanna telepathically ascertained that Michael had recently been "abducted" or, in Inanna's terms, taken for a ride on the Mother Ship with the Etherians. Inanna also recognized Clarissa as a multidimensional self of the Lady of the Garnets, a close friend to Inanna from the Pleiadian star system. And Michael was the multidimensional self of the Commander, husband to the Lady of the Garnets.

Inanna was thrilled by this exciting love story. She thought, *How brave of my dear friends to incarnate as these two and fearlessly face the perilous third dimension to assist in liberating the human species.*

Noting the resemblance between this beautiful young girl and the Lady of the Garnets, Inanna spoke affectionately to Clarissa.

"Your splendid red hair reminds me of an old and cherished friend, someone I love very much."

Clarissa felt happy. She couldn't imagine what she had been so worried about; she felt just fine. Everything was working out the way it was meant to be; surely, she had known that all along.

Gracie saw Clarissa happily smiling, and so pressed Inanna for an answer.

"She wants to know if her Michael is okay."

Inanna was curious to see what the Commander might be up to in the body of a young twentieth-century American male, so she concentrated her focus on the ancient ruins of Machu Picchu. There she saw, standing high on a hill, a slender figure with very long black hair; he wore no shirt and was lifting his arms as the sun began to rise behind him.

Inanna watched with a passionate interest. As the wind whispered through the mountain ruins, the Commander appeared in the first rays of the dawn to his multidimensional self, Michael.

Seeing that Clarissa's lover was in the best of care, Inanna returned to her girls. No time had passed.

"I can promise you that no harm has or will come to Michael. He will be home soon to hold you safely in his arms once again. Now, in the meantime," Inanna suggested, "I invite you to join me on an illuminating journey. Gracie will join us and, who knows, probably a few more. I know someone who loves you and wants to see you."

A little adventure sounded very appealing to Clarissa just now. She had been rather envious when Michael was abducted by those perfectly nice aliens and taken on a marvelous spaceship without her; and then he'd immediately gone off to Machu Picchu while she had to stay home. No wonder she was miserable.

"I'd love to go!" she replied confidently.

IV

DINNER

Inanna sat across the candlelit table from Jehran. She was falling helplessly into his eyes, and simultaneously monitoring Gracie and Clarissa. At the last moment, Inanna had decided to wear a revealing evening gown with matching jewels. She looked gorgeous; and even though she wasn't really hungry, the dinner menu was tempting. Inanna secretly wondered if she could possibly have imagined anyone as perfect as Jehran. Ah, her life was good these days; perhaps that *Wall* thing was lifting after all.

Jehran had whisked her away in his private spacecraft, an amorphous vehicle with no mechanical controls whatsoever, that responded solely to his mental commands. The ship was solid and yet not solid; Jehran's thoughts could alter the form and velocity of his ship. He had decided to take Inanna to a nearby planet whose orbiting moon contained a unique restaurant. The dining rooms were underground; their interiors were programmed as holograms at the individual request of each patron. From space above, the moon looked empty and desolate; but inside the elaborate underground tunnels, an intimate network of luxury and fantasy displayed every imaginable dining taste in the Universe.

Jehran had pre-selected for Inanna the period of early Sumer on the planet Earth. He hoped it would please her to be in the familiar surroundings she had once been happy in, before her cousin Marduk had taken over the planet and destroyed her temples.

"Jehran, this is wonderful. It looks just like my palace in the old days. How imaginative of you!" Inanna looked around at the hanging flower gardens of hyacinth and jasmine, floors of lapis lazuli and turquoise, and rows of gilded statuary lions. She and Jehran were seated in an open pavilion surrounded by tall malachite columns. The air was soft, warm and fragrant. Moonlight bathed the two lovers in a gentle radiance as Jehran moved his hand across the pure white tablecloth toward hers.

"Whatever I can do, pretty lady, to please you brings happiness to me. We will be as one — one heart and one mind."

For the first time in many a year, Inanna, uncharacteristically, blushed like a schoolgirl. She knew what he said was true; they were to become as one. What she was feeling was changing her; everything felt new to her. She had learned to find happiness entirely within herself, and now she was to share the *self* she had become with another.

"Inanna," Jehran began, "I would like you to come with me to my home. On the way, we would stop at the planet Valthezon where for the past few galactic years I have been the acting Minister of Finance and Trade. I have some business to complete there before I return to my home planet. I believe you will enjoy the experience, and I want you with me."

"Valthezon! In all the Galaxy, the finest chocolates are produced there. I have enjoyed more than a few of these delicacies in my time. My great-grandmother, Antu, served *only* chocolates from Valthezon at her celebrated parties. I would love to go there," Inanna replied excitedly.

"Before we can actually enter into the dimensional frequencies of my home planet," Jehran explained, "we will have to mutate your existing cellular structure somewhat. With all my heart, I feel you are ready for this modification and that such a small conversion will not prove too arduous for you. I would never do anything to harm you. I have been watching your life for a long time now with great interest."

Good lord! Inanna winced. *Oh dear, I guess he knows everything about me; all my ex-husbands and lovers, and all those dreadful wars I waged on Earth. Telepathy has its drawbacks!*

"Do not be alarmed, dear lady; I do not judge you for your adventures. I was referring rather to your recent bravery, and to the success you have attained in helping your multidimensional selves to activate their latent DNA. I myself was once involved in such a learning process and experienced a similar set of circumstances. This kind of thing happens all the time, you know."

"It does?" Inanna asked incredulously. She could not believe that other members of the Intergalactic Federation had also been so unwise as to mutate the DNA of an entire race of beings and use them as slave workers. Her family had acted irresponsibly, and surely there was no one in the Universe as naughty and unruly as her cousin Marduk.

"Yes, lovely one, the experience of tyranny is quite common in this Universe. Who is to stop Prime Creator's creator gods from occasionally following their own selfish whims to their ultimate conclusion? They must move through experience in order to learn.

"Eventually, all tyrants will evolve past the overwhelming need to control everything and everyone in their paths. Life is a grand adventure for us all and I have behaved just as you have; I love you all the more for your great passion for life. I especially love the brave and forthright way you have taken the destiny of the human race into your heart, and dedicated yourself to its rescue."

"And to my own as well!" said Inanna. "Don't forget *The Wall* which surrounded us and prevented our evolution, including mine. I had never known how dreadful boredom could be, and I never want to know again."

Jehran smiled at her. "Yes, Prime Creator is not fond of stagnation. The river of life is ever in motion, flowing eternally outward, onward, and back again to its source. It is the infinite joy of our experiences that beckons Prime Creator to endlessly veil Itself in us. Eternally playing hide-and-seek with Itself, the Source becomes lost in Its creation—and then remembers once again."

Inanna melted; his words were sweeter to her ears than any music she had ever heard. He was everything she had ever dreamed of, and wise beyond any man she had ever known. She couldn't imagine being any happier.

Jehran gently caressed her hand, saying, "And so, pretty lady, will you come home with me?"

"I would love to."

"Then, it is settled. What would you like for dinner?"

✳

Michael shivered as a warrior from another time and place materialized in the sun's early-morning rays. Before his eyes stood the Commander, the same being who had taken him aboard the enormous Mother Ship orbiting just beyond Saturn.

Michael spoke to his vision. "I have kept my promise—I have come to this place to be with you."

The Commander answered him. "I am your friend, and I am also that which you are. Here we appear as separate beings, but in another dimension, we are as one. Do not fear me, for there is no need for fear. I am here to serve your evolution, and, through you, the evolution of the human species."

Michael was in awe, but he was not afraid. He remembered how kind the Commander had been to him on the Mother Ship, and he wondered where his beautiful wife, the Lady of the Garnets, might be this fine morning. She reminded Michael of his own Clarissa, for they both had copper-red hair.

The Commander changed the subject. "Michael, have you not wondered how the human species came to endure this ceaseless repetition of birth and death, pleasure and pain, and the endlessly destructive wars of greedy tyrants? Longing to free yourself from the limitations of the material world, do you not wonder why it seems so difficult for your species to evolve?"

"Yes, I have sought answers to the confinement of my species, but to no avail," Michael said.

"Then I bring you a vision. Sit down, my son, and I will show you a period of your history that has been kept secret from you for far too long."

40

As the Commander opened the Eye of Michael's Mind, the ancient ruins surrounding them unveiled holographic memories. In the skies above them, many spaceships of various sizes and shapes landed and took off from Machu Picchu. Long lines of slaves loaded the ships with gold. Their overseers were not human, but a mix of alien races whose skin was either pale blue or a scaly light green. They were dressed magnificently in dark blue military uniforms trimmed with gold and lapis ornaments. The aliens were not openly cruel to their captives; rather, it was as though the slaves knew no other way of living beyond this ceaseless drudgery, and thus they worked on obediently. Service to their creators was their only experience. The sight of such a limited existence made Michael shudder.

The Commander then showed him another vision. In the Eye of his Mind, Michael saw a genetic laboratory where a male, *Homo erectus,* a wild creature from the savannas of Earth, was imprisoned. He had been captured for his DNA; his captors worked to fuse his genes with those of an alien species, who were of Pleiadian and Sirian origin. Michael saw the product of these genetic manipulations become the prototype of the perfect worker, designed solely to serve these extraterrestrials. The slave race was created to dig in the mines in order to extract gold and other precious metals for the depleted atmosphere of the artificial planet, Nibiru.

So, Michael thought, *it is all true.* He and all the human species were nothing more than a race of slave workers who had been bred to labor in a mining colony on the periphery of this Galaxy. Michael had read books and heard people discuss such incredible stories as this, but he hadn't really believed them. Just as he hadn't really believed in UFOs until he was abducted and led through the corridors of the Mother

Ship with his new friend and mentor, the Commander.

Michael sighed and sat down on a large stone.

"Yes, my son, it is the grievous truth," the Commander replied. "But now is the time to change, to set yourself free. In doing so, you will contribute to the transmission of truth across the planet. Truth has the power to activate latent genetic codes. When they *know*, many will begin to abandon the claws of tyranny once and for all. This is why I have asked you to come here, to experience for yourself the hidden history of this ancient place and your planet.

"Michael, you are more than your body, more than this vulnerable flesh and blood, more than the rich earth you are made from. You are a part of Prime Creator, and you are a part of me. If you so choose, you can reactivate your own DNA and help this entire planet find its way back to its destined path of evolution. You can be as powerful as you need be; you can conquer the chains of tyranny within yourself. And I will help you, if you but ask me."

Michael stood up and began to walk in circles. He felt so many things at once; he was both angry and ecstatic. His body was burning with energy. Staring up at the cold blue sky, he lifted his fist and cried out in anguish. His voice echoed through the empty walls of the ancient ruins and down into the silent valleys below. As that one cry broke loose from the depths of his soul, Michael embodied all the men and women of the human race who had ever lost hope. And as that cry slipped from his being, Michael changed. The cells in his slim hard youthful body began to mutate and a golden light surrounded him.

Michael fell to the cold ground; his body was mutating very quickly. In a matter of moments he reviewed every lifetime he had ever spent on planet Earth, as well as the other lifetimes he had experienced in other dimensions and other forms. He saw himself a slave in chains, beaten and dragging huge stones. He tasted the blood of war in the heartless armies that rampaged through time; as a soldier he burned villages, murdered men, and raped women.

In the Eye of his Mind he saw himself burning alive in a small farmhouse, along with the woman he loved and their children. He observed the repetitious and senseless oblivion in the cycle of yet another war, another army. He had been victim and victor; both experiences had left him empty, feeling nothing.

Lifetime after lifetime, Michael repeated the endless cycles of birth and death, passions and sorrows, and he wondered why. What did it all mean? Why did he not learn from his past? Why did he make the same mistakes over and over? Why was he bound ever to foolishly repeat the past?

Michael knew now that he wanted change more than anything in the world. He knew that without it, his life—even with Clarissa—was doomed to the same sad futility that he had already fully experienced.

The Commander lovingly placed his hand on Michael's burning forehead. "My son, it is enough for one day. Walk down into the village and eat something. Go and be healed, and know that I love you. Your bravery here today has earned my lasting respect. Go now, eat and be well."

Michael opened his human eyes to find himself alone on the windy hill. He didn't feel brave; he felt tired and hungry, and it was getting cold and dark. What had happened to his body? He felt different. Confused and drained, he wandered down the hill thinking that anything would taste good to him in this moment.

43

V

WORMHOLE

Within all-the-possible worlds and beyond all time, Thel Dar floated in a sea of undifferentiated Beingness.

Gazing around 360 degrees, Thel Dar lovingly moved focus from one dimension to another. From this perspective each aspect of Life appeared as an extraordinary masterpiece of perfection. From the great forever of the indigo Void and on into the Light, the infinite polarities of every dimensional level pushed and probed one another in an endless variety of velocities generating the vast expressions of Prime Creator.

For the pleasure of pure motion, Thel Dar rolled over and over; rainbows of iridescent photons flowed from the rolling motion in cascades of energy and frequencies of joy. Creation *is*; and floating around in the Mind of Prime Creator, Thel Dar felt the contentment of unending bliss in the movement of energy spilling out into all-the-possible worlds.

Focusing on its multidimensional selves, Thel Dar felt around for Inanna and Gracie. Clarissa, a multidimensional self of the Lady of the Garnets, was with the girls. Thel Dar could feel Inanna, Gracie, and Clarissa moving their consciousness toward the place Thel Dar floated within. Being both male and female, Thel Dar enjoyed appearing as a great mother goddess to Inanna and Gracie, who were two parts of itself. Thinking of the girls, Thel Dar smiled—and Love, as energy, flowed out into all-the-possible worlds.

Inanna was evolving very nicely. Lately Thel Dar had emitted sweet melodies through Inanna, who took pleasure in playing a lute for Jehran, her lover. Thel Dar was happy that Inanna had at long last found a lover worthy of her—or, from another point of view, that she had become worthy of Jehran. Their sublime lovemaking was increasing energy levels in Thel Dar and all of its multidimensional selves in all-the-possible worlds.

Thel Dar in fact had no name, but the multidimensional selves needed to have some sound for the purpose of recognition. Not all of its selves referred to this vast Being as Thel Dar, but Inanna and Gracie seemed to be especially fond of the name. To them it meant having the will and the courage to know. Thel Dar knew its multidimensional selves attached a great deal of importance to making distinctions within the polarities, and therefore attempted to accommodate them, even though from the perspective of the forever Void—everything was truth.

No one specific name could contain Thel Dar, who had many, many names and many forms. He/she had been manifesting its *Self* as any and every imaginable probability for as long as memory had existed. Thel Dar had been the Void itself, a star, a comet, a planet, a forest, and countless polarities of beings in all-the-possible worlds. At this moment, Thel Dar was now many of these expressions: dragon and king, slave and fairy, deer and dwarf; Pleiadian, reptilian, earthling, Arcturian, and one of the little Greys, as well as many others.

Life is vast, and Thel Dar loved all of creation and everything in it, enjoying all of its selves, in all of its expressions. Thel Dar did not judge creation, but rather sought only to live it; to *be* it in its fullest.

Thel Dar felt Inanna's intention to bring Gracie and Clarissa into the forever Void, and so projected a corridor of thought toward the lovable blue lady. Inanna felt the familiar gentle warmth that told her Thel Dar was creating an opening—a wormhole in time, so to speak, which would direct their consciousness to move easily through the veils of dimensional levels. Inanna picked up the vision of the wormhole as Thel Dar's love flow in and over her. Then, in thought, Inanna directed the two women, who sat in a house in the Pacific Northwest on planet Earth, to close their eyes and *become* the stillness that was permeating Gracie's living room.

Gracie and Clarissa saw in the Eye of their Mind a long, winding, golden tunnel open before them. Clarissa gasped; Gracie reached out and touched her new friend's hand reassuringly. All was still again. Then all three felt themselves drawn up into this tunnel by a powerful magnetic force. Inanna knew that the magnetic pull was nothing other than the great love Thel Dar felt for them. Inanna was happy.

In another part of her Universe, on a spaceship moving toward the planet Valthezon, Inanna lay on a blue velvet bed with her head in Jehran's lap. Jehran was telling her amusing stories about the customs on the planets to which he had been ambassador. Inanna herself knew how much fun it was to hop all over the Universe visiting different cultures, learning from and about them, and she was glad Jehran was so intelligent and well-traveled.

Creation was wonderfully diverse and fantastic. There were many more interesting things to do in this world than argue and wage wars, as her family, the family of Anu, had done on the planet Earth for what now seemed an eternity to her. How could she have been so small-minded as to have taken pleasure in war and conquest? The limited frequency spectrum of tyranny was for adolescents; Inanna was relieved to have outgrown it, and a little embarrassed by her memories.

Jehran caressed her forehead; feeling her thoughts, he reassured her. "My darling Inanna, do not feel less than anyone in creation. This phase, known as *the understanding of tyrants*, has been experienced by all who were brave enough to descend into the lower dimensions. The lower regions allow and facilitate such adventures. Think of all you have learned, all you now know, and all you have transmitted into the Mind of Prime Creator."

Inanna sighed. Yes, life in the electromagnetic frequency prisons of tyrants was sweetly sad at best, and often ended in bitter tragedy.

Once again Jehran read her mind—or, rather, her heart.

"Emotions are the most powerful communicators and catalysts in the Universe," he said. "Because the essence of Prime Creator and all of creation is Love, emotions are the transducers of experience. The ability to have powerful feelings is the greatest gift of Life. This is why the race known as the Greys are trying so desperately to improve their genomes, for, sadly, they can no longer feel. Mind is not everything; it is a receptor and storage facilitator which makes useful, infinite, unending distinctions. But the capacity to feel Love is truly the source of creative power and the underlying matrix of all Life."

Inanna snuggled herself closer to this man whom she adored with all her heart. He was so warm, and he smelled so good to her, so very *male* in contrast to her femaleness. Inanna found their intense intimacy intoxicating; loving Jehran was wonderful. Lifting herself up a little, she wrapped her creamy blue arms around his neck and kissed his lips. As she drifted into a sea of passion, Inanna became aware that part of herself was being called to visit the exquisite radiant-light Being, Thel Dar, who floated in another kind of sea, one of undifferentiated Beingness. Inanna kissed Jehran more deeply, and split her awareness between these two realities, as she felt drawn into the wormhole.

VI

BROKEN HEARTS

Michael stared vacantly at his half-eaten plate of rice and beans. He had barely even tasted the food as he wolfed it down. His stomach felt unsettled. The beans had been laced with red-hot peppers, and his mouth was on fire. He reached for a cold beer and consumed it in one long gulping motion, then ordered another.

In the Eye of his Mind, he saw the spaceships landing again and again at Machu Picchu. Michael was still in a mild state of shock as he struggled to absorb the information the Pleiadian Commander had given him.

The human species was a genetically engineered worker race created by a bunch of avaricious aliens who wanted to extract gold from this planet, his planet, Earth. Or at least he *thought* it was his planet; perhaps, Michael reflected, I too come from some other place in this Universe. From childhood on, he had been an avid reader of science fiction and had loved anything having to do with space travel.

He thought of Clarissa; how could he tell her what he now knew? Would she understand? Deep in his heart, Michael felt she was too dependent on him. It was as if she wanted him to bring life to her, and sometimes that pressure made him want to run away from her.

Staring at the spicy beans, and waiting for a second cold beer, he recalled everything he had learned. He felt angry, perplexed, and somehow relieved all at the same time. At least he now knew the truth, or a part of it. The Earth was trapped in a sort of frequency prison, partially because the human genome wasn't fully connected—in fact had been purposefully left malfunctioning—and partly because the prevailing electromagnetic frequencies actually *prevented* people from reactivating the unused parts of their brains. Michael knew that something called *The Wave* was coming to Earth from a race of beings known as the Etherians. This *Wave* of high frequencies acted like an antidote for those humans who wanted freedom from their limitations. Michael knew that he was a part of this process, and more than anything else, he wanted to activate his own latent DNA.

Inanna, Gracie, and Clarissa allowed themselves to be pulled into the golden wormhole Thel Dar had spun for them. At the same time, Inanna sensed the presence of another of her multidimensional selves. It was, of course, Olnwynn, who had an uncanny knack for intruding upon especially exciting realities. When a great adventure was about to take place, he invariably arrived ready for action, as if he had a sixth sense.

As the four slid down-or-up the wormhole, Olnwynn began laughing, and the girls joined him. This was better than a roller coaster. They all felt happy; wormholes were fun!

At some point in the tunnel, an open space appeared —and there in the blackness stood a magnificent mahogany grand piano. Divine melodies flowed forth from its keys. Everyone slowed down, moving toward the great instrument to see who or what was playing it. There, seated on an oversized bench, was a small man who had the look of a mischievous child. He wore a stylish white wig and a silk suit trimmed with lace.

"Hello," he said. "I am Wolfgang Amadeus Mozart. 'Wolfie' to those who love me."

Gracie could scarcely believe her eyes; she was thrilled. Mozart had always been her favorite composer. His music had lifted her to pure states of rapture, and on lonely nights she had often secretly wished that she had been born in his time and had been his wife, or at least his lover. She was convinced that his life would have been far better with her in it; he would never have died so young and poor. She would have treasured his person as much as his music. It was a sweet fantasy for her lonely moments.

All three girls were immediately charmed by Wolfie, as he insisted they call him. He was boyish, cute, and funny. He made rude jokes that were gross but innocent, and they could not help but laugh. Olnwynn noticed how quickly all three of the girls warmed up to little Wolfie.

"So, Wolfie Mozart," Olnwynn laughed, "I can see you have a real way with the ladies."

At this opening, Wolfie began to go on and on about his sexual conquests among the women of his day. Such an outpouring suggested that it had been a long time since Herr Mozart had found a suitably interested listener. Beginning with his female students, he proceeded to enumerate his conquests of the ladies in the royal court. Naturally, Olnwynn was enthralled and threw in a few tid-bits of his own; after all, he had enjoyed a similar talent in his own life and time.

Inanna, Gracie, and Clarissa soon tired of hearing how many women these two charming rogues had seduced, and began to remember why they were in the wormhole tunnel in the first place, and where they were headed. Inanna suggested that Olnwynn stay with his new friend; he could catch up with them later. As the girls moved on, Gracie turned to look back at Wolfie, her imaginary love; he was everything she had ever wanted in a man. The thought of all the beautiful music he had written and his charming, humorous ways made him irresistible to her. She reluctantly waved good-bye.

Moving on through the tunnel, Inanna, Gracie, and Clarissa came to a vast opening which at first appeared to be nothing but an empty indigo darkness. But as they emerged into this inky void, they noticed a geometric grid of thin laser-beam-like lines of light. These lines formed a Merkabah—two pyramids which fit into each other, one pointed in one direction and the other in its opposite. The girls were in Thel Dar's Merkabah, and it was enormous. Subtle neon lines of light faded off and on, defining the Merkabah which provided the base for structure in the vast rich blackness of the forever Void.

The glorious radiant-light Being Thel Dar stood before them, and the sight of such beauty took Clarissa's breath away. Her heart beating rapidly, she sat down next to Inanna and Gracie on nothing but empty space; there was no floor, nor any down nor up for that matter, only a kind of *forever darkness* that felt scary but familiar. Sitting in the half-lotus position, she found herself floating in measureless blackness. It was almost comical.

Clarissa could not find it in herself to stay afraid; the radiant-light Being who stood before them was obviously the most loving energy she had ever encountered. Clarissa had never before experienced this combination of intense power and gentleness. It made her giddy; she had never felt so loved by anyone. She thought, *It must be true; God is Love.*

Gracie recalled the first time she had ever met this Being. In the cedar forest on Lost Mountain, Thel Dar had appeared to her on a warm sunny afternoon that felt like only yesterday to Gracie. Linear Earth time was losing its grip on her. Here in this vast place of dark promise, she understood that time did not exist. Time was merely the result of thought being projected onto empty space in varying frequencies.

The darkness did not frighten Gracie; she remembered how seeds sprouted and grew in the darkness of the Earth's rich black soil. She had always told her friends that she was not afraid of the night, because "dark is where the seeds grow." This indigo ocean felt like a blanket wrapping itself around her, a blanket filled with promise.

Inanna listened to Gracie's thoughts, and was delighted to see the girl expanding her consciousness into the forever Void and toward the understanding of no-time.

Inanna also began to recall her first meeting with Thel Dar. It had occurred when Inanna had lost everything she had loved and created on the planet Earth, including her husband Sargon and their magical kingdom, Akkad. Open to any possible understanding of her defeat and anguish, Inanna had desperately wanted to know why there had to be so much suffering, and what she could do to heal the broken pieces of herself.

Thel Dar had shown Inanna a powerful love, explaining to her that she and Thel Dar were in fact one and the same; and that Inanna had always been loved, even when she had foolishly hurt herself. Inanna had then remembered that she had always been a gatherer of information and experience for Prime Creator; that she was intimately connected to this radiant-light Being, who in turn was a part of Prime Creator. In some way, they were all interconnected, nested one within the other in consciousness, like skins of an onion or the little Russian dolls made on Earth. Ultimately they were all One—one consciousness, one Being formed from Love. Everything in creation was connected to and a part of everything else.

For Inanna, this knowledge had been healing and exhilarating at the same time. It gave her the courage and the desire to descend to Earth in human form as her various multidimensional selves, one of whom was, of course, Gracie. And now the two, Gracie and Inanna, had brought their new friend Clarissa here to meet Thel Dar.

Turning to Clarissa and assessing the state of her heart and her confusion, Thel Dar spoke sweetly. "You may call me Thel Dar if it pleases you."

Clarissa began to cry. Thel Dar's tenderness was melting her into a pool of tears.

"Little girl, you carry great sorrow within you. Your lover has abandoned you in his search for truth in a distant land. Believe me, Clarissa, he will return to you. You must find strength within yourself. External happiness is a measure of one's internal reality. As you find the courage to become sovereign and to rely on your own inner resources, you will find that love will come to you on many levels and in many ways. Quite mysteriously, Michael will simply want to return home to you."

Clarissa cried, "But does Michael want me to be, like you said, that 'sovereign' thing? I don't know what he wants me to be."

Thel Dar smiled. "The question is *not* what he wants you to be. The question is, *who are you?* What do you want to be? You must first be yourself and love that *self* that is within you; then there will be no emptiness to frighten him away. He will love you, for you will be whole, complete within yourself, deserving of his respect, and magnetizing his undying love. You can easily stand together when you have learned to stand alone."

Even though this sounded like a contradiction to Clarissa's mind, her heart felt the truth in what this beautiful creature of light was saying to her. After all, it was Michael's spirit of independence, his ability to think for himself, and his love of knowledge that had made Clarissa fall so deeply in love with him in the first place. He was the missing part of herself. If she felt that way about him, wouldn't he want the same from her? Wouldn't he be attracted by a confident woman who trusted in herself?

Something shifted in Clarissa's consciousness; she grew, expanding herself mysteriously, and by osmosis her expansion affected and enhanced Inanna, Gracie, and also Thel Dar.

Miraculously, Clarissa's broken heart began to heal as she determined from that moment forward to change the way she thought about herself. She made up her mind never to cling to Michael again, nor to demand that he fill her emptiness, even if that clinging was occasionally sweet. She would learn to love and respect herself, and thus gain Michael's love and respect.

Far away in South America, Michael sat reflecting on his empty plate and his indigestion. In the exact moment that Clarissa embraced her new understanding, Michael felt a terrible longing to go home. Suddenly he missed her. Finishing off the last of his beer, he headed for the train which would take him to Lima and the airport, and back to the USA and his Clarissa.

VII

THE PLANE RIDE

Michael, fast asleep on the airplane, dreamed that he was surrounded by little Grey aliens in an underground facility. The creature assigned to Michael was leading him around, showing him the incubators filled with a variety of crossbred babies and very small children who were half human and half Grey.

Michael stared into the enormous black eyes of his tour guide to read its sad thoughts. Over the eons, the little Greys had lost the ability to feel. They had so fervently revered the powers of the mind that they had unwittingly bred their connection to the heart right out of their DNA. They had not realized what was happening to them, nor how terrible the consequences would be, until it was too late.

Only a few Greys had noticed and had begged their leaders to do something to stop the ominous direction of their evolution. These few had understood that the heart opens the door to Prime Creator and the secrets of Life, but no one had listened to them. Most among their culture had fully embraced the idea that the only valuable knowledge was that gained through the mind.

Their bodies, including their sexual organs, likewise had withered away from lack of use. As they learned to communicate telepathically, mind to mind, their mouths all but disappeared and they learned to feed themselves chemical nutrients through their skin.

One day, they realized that they had reached an impasse in their evolution. They had built a virtual prison for themselves in their own dimension of time and space; they were trapped. Without their feelings, they could no longer access the heart center and shift themselves into the higher dimensional frequencies.

Realizing their tragic plight, they looked around the Universe for a species they had some genetic connection with, which still retained the capacity to feel. There on the edge of a galaxy was a remote planet called Terra, which for eons had been little more than a mining outpost used mainly by the wily Nibiruans. Long before the Pleiadians of Nibiru had invaded Terra, the ancient ancestors of the Greys had set up a small colony there. Experimentation with the natives' genetics had left enough of their DNA in Terra's population to facilitate their again interbreeding with the present species of humans.

Michael wasn't afraid of his gentle guide. The vacant sadness in his large dark eyes made Michael feel a compassion and sympathy for this small alien creature. However shocking the odd forms of the unique new breed of babies and children were, Michael felt love for them. How could he find it in his heart to call these children ugly, even if at first sight they appeared abnormal to him? After all, they were all a part of God.

✳

The flight attendant pulled down Michael's tray and placed a hot plate of preservatives, otherwise known as food, in front of him. Michael looked at the display of modern chemical achievements in wonder. This was food? The smell of additive-laced chicken and lasagna mildly sickened him. *Oh, well,* he thought. *I'll drink the soda.*

Michael closed his eyes, remembering what he had just seen in his dream. A lot of things were going on in this crazy world that weren't being discussed in the media. Now and then there were a few televised interviews of people who had seen UFOs, or who had been abducted; but these programs always gave the professional debunkers the last word, leaving the people who dared to believe in such things feeling like fools.

What were the established media so afraid of? Why couldn't they just tell the public the truth? Would the truth really drive people to stop paying taxes or overthrow the state? Most governments were already in chaos, with public and private debt mounting everywhere. Everyone knew something had definitely gone wrong.

Many people were terrified by the thought of alien races invading Earth. Images of reptilians devouring humans arose in the subconscious mind of man from the primordial cellular fear of dragons and dinosaurs. Tales of cattle mutilations and forced abductions served to exacerbate horror in the human imagination. Day by day the stories became more complex. Earth's sky was thick with alien craft.

Michael thought of the Commander, and once again his friend appeared in his consciousness.

Speaking to Michael's mind, the Commander began. "The concept that there are no 'bad' alien races is far too radical for the average human mind to embrace. In truth, there are only a multitude of *other* races who live throughout the galaxies. Some simply have a very different perspective than the humans, and some have conflicting ideas on what Earth humans are useful for.

"I imagine that you have eaten the meat of a sweet young lamb, have you not? And someone, somewhere slaughtered that lamb, not looking into its eyes or noticing its innocent beauty, so that you could have its flesh on your plate with mint sauce. And you think nothing of that; you think that's fine.

"Perhaps, from the little lamb's point of view, you might be observed as a 'bad' alien. In the Mind of Prime Creator, there is only creation, and all in it simply *is*, and has the right to pursue its own destiny as much as you do."

Michael thought about it. He supposed that if he were that little Grey he would do everything he could to save his own family, his own species. But why didn't the aliens just tell the people of Earth what they wanted, and try to make agreements? Or was our own government hiding the truth in order to hold on to what was left of its power?

The flight attendant removed the untouched food and Michael reached into his backpack for some dried raisins. He had grown thin in Peru. It would be good to indulge in Clarissa's home cooking and put on a few pounds. Reluctantly, he thought of the little lamb and tried to remember how many tender morsels of its meat he might have eaten during his young life. Let's see, there was that year in England where everyone ate lamb on Sundays, and those shish kebab things he had gotten a taste for in Greece. His mind balked; he didn't really want to know, and besides, that wasn't the Commander's point. The point was various points of view, perspectives in a relative world.

Back on Jehran's spaceship, Inanna was enjoying a blue bubble bath. The bubbles were fun; she idly built little castles and tunnels through them. Jehran entered the room and smiled at his beloved and her lavish beauty.

"Inanna, my dear, soon we'll arrive on Valthezon. There we'll be greeted by the local governor and his wife; we'll tour the planet to observe how well the suggestions I made have been implemented. I think you will enjoy yourself. Valthezon's trade and economics are based on a wonderful system; indeed, their wealth is founded on the presence of a commodity virtually invisible to them all."

Inanna, touching the gold and lapis necklace that adorned her pretty neck, thought how visibly solid the ornament felt to her at that moment. She was still very fond of her jewels and her comfort.

Jehran answered her thoughts. "That is fine, my darling girl." Changing the subject, he asked. "Shall I join you in your bath, or do you prefer your solitude?"

Inanna smiled and answered by pulling back a blanket of blue bubbles to make room for her lover. There would be plenty of time later for talk of economics and trade; for now, there was the magic of their love.

Jehran had known from the first moment he had

looked into her eyes that Inanna possessed the genetic capacity to transmute her physical body into the realms of higher frequencies. Jehran knew that in order to travel to his home, Inanna would have to master the task of shifting her cellular structure beyond the frequency of light. Through the focus of her consciousness, she would become *hyper-luminal*.

He knew she was capable of such a transition, and he looked forward to initiating her into the higher dimensions through the passionate fusion of their abundant energies. The sexual experience wasn't essential to achieving a frequency transformation; many became hyper-luminal solely through enhancing their own consciousness, and without the delicious arts of lovemaking. But those who did experience such frequency shifts through sexual union, counted them among the best remembrances in their data banks, a sort of not-to-be-missed when-it-comes-your-way thing. And Inanna had definitely come Jehran's way. It was just a matter of a little more time now. He could wait.

VIII

SCHOOL

Back in the wormhole, Thel Dar revealed to Clarissa that just as Gracie was one of Inanna's multidimensional selves, Clarissa shared the same kind of alliance with the Lady of the Garnets. Clarissa was a projected portional *self* of this red-haired beauty from the Pleiades.

Clarissa recalled that when she was a child, a beautiful lady with long copper hair like hers had sung sweet dream songs to her. She had long ago forgotten all about these dreams; but now as Thel Dar spoke, images came clearly into her mind. Clarissa resolved to seek out this Lady of the Garnets.

"That will be easy, little one," Thel Dar said. "She has been patiently waiting for you to notice her your whole life. Even now, she is waiting to guide you and help you reactivate your latent DNA."

Then Thel Dar and Inanna explained to Clarissa that when Inanna's family had created the human race so long ago, they had purposefully left the genetic codes of the human species functioning at less than a hundred percent. Inanna filled in the details as Thel Dar explained the far-reaching consequences of these foolish actions. Inanna and the Lady of the Garnets were both working to help all human beings gain their freedom, and the future was looking a lot brighter because of people like Gracie and Clarissa. There was definitely hope out there; things were happening.

"So, are you the one who sent *The Wave* we have heard so much about?" asked Clarissa.

"No, *The Wave* is a gift from the Etherians," answered Inanna.

"My, there are so many groups and races in the Universe; I suspect I'm just beginning to learn about only a few."

"That is so, Clarissa," Thel Dar replied. "But think of all the unknowns and all the adventures that lie before you. Life is limitless in its expression. You are just beginning to live."

"Why was all this kept from us for so long?" Clarissa inquired.

"Well, that is a long story," Inanna responded. "But if you want me to, I will give you some answers."

Clarissa nodded, and Inanna began to explain how her cousin Marduk and his tyrants had gained control over the Earth by augmenting the fears of human beings and feeding off of them.

"The humans were conditioned to believe that God was external to them, and that they were born as sinners who must worship the one god. Well, it is true, in a sense, that there is only one god; there is a totality of creation manifested as multiple universes within the Mind of God. There are also as many Prime Creators as there are universes. And ultimately all is one, a Oneness that enfolds all the creations of all-the-possible worlds.

"But the one who commanded the humans to bow down and worship him was in fact an extraterrestrial from a more advanced technology whose zealous ambition was to enslave the humans to serve him. He was equally ambitious to subdue the other gods, who were in fact his own family, the family of Anu. This ambitious tyrant god is my cousin, Lord Marduk," Inanna concluded.

Watching Clarissa's furrowed brow, Thel Dar added, "My dear, think of it as a game. Prime Creator separates itself in various parts and then plays, testing itself against itself, generating the eternal dance of creation."

To bring the conversation a little more down to earth, Gracie took over.

"If we humans had known all along how many other worlds and beings there were out there, we would never have become enslaved. Knowing that life was infinite, we would have ignored such ultimatums and moved on to new adventures in all-the-possible worlds. This Marduk guy started brainwashing us with his intense style of propaganda, and our half-wired DNA did the rest.

"By the twentieth century," Gracie continued, "there was so much subliminal programming and propaganda coming at us from television and other media that most people lost the ability to think for themselves. The tyrants placed electromagnetic grids all over the planet to entrain and trap our frequencies in a very limited spectrum. We only use ten or fifteen percent of our brains; people just couldn't fight it."

Clarissa took a deep breath and sighed. Placing her head in her hands, she realized she was exhausted. Gracie glanced at Inanna; it was enough for one day. Thel Dar waved good-bye to the travelers, and in thought, whisked them down the long tunnel. In a wormhole minute, the three girls found themselves back in Gracie's living room.

A few minutes later, Olnwynn and Wolfie popped out of the wormhole after them.

"We were looking for you," said Olnwynn.

Gracie walked Clarissa to the front door, recommending that she go home and get some sleep. Gracie was sure that Michael would return soon, and Clarissa had a lot to think about. Clarissa thanked Gracie for a wonderful day and headed home exhausted.

Inanna was still aware of what was going on in the blue bubble bath between her and Jehran back on his spaceship; and so she excused herself for awhile, leaving Gracie with her multidimensional self and guardian, Olnwynn, and his new friend, Wolfie.

Gracie entreated Wolfie to play her modest piano, but Wolfie demurred; in his non-physical body, he explained, he couldn't make the keys move.

But wait, he had an idea; for a short time he could borrow Gracie's body, her hands and feet, to play his music for her.

Gracie was delighted; she sat down in front of the black-and-white keys and closed her eyes. From a little house in the Pacific Northwest, Wolfgang Amadeus Mozart once again filled the air with his timeless harmonies of pure beauty.

✶

At home that night, Clarissa slept soundly. The bed didn't seem so big and she felt happier than she had since Michael left. Around five o'clock in the morning, a travel-weary Michael crawled into bed with her and wrapped himself around her. The two lovers began to cry, softly and sweetly, until they both fell fast asleep in each other's arms.

IX

THE MAGIC TOUCH

Blue bubbles were still floating on the warm waters as Jehran slipped out of his silken robes and into the marble bath with his beloved, Inanna. Inanna sighed as Jehran began to touch her gently, slowly moving his hands over her firm, voluptuous body. Relaxing, she rolled her eyes up to watch a beautiful light display within the Eye of her Mind.

Fantastic lights sprayed across the vast darkness in the top of her head, sometimes as showers of rainbow colors, and sometimes as phosphorescent, dancing geometric patterns. These lights were hypnotic and lovely.

As Jehran continued to touch her, she felt every nerve, every cell in her body heightened by his caress. She felt each atom within her sing as it joyfully increased the speed of its spin. For a moment, Inanna opened her eyes to her lover and smiled.

Jehran lifted her up out of the warm waters and onto a soft white towel spread on the lapis tiles. As he continued to raise the frequencies of her body, his hands became more highly charged with electrical energy, *chi*. His lips burned with desire and his body, in unison with hers, followed her changing frequencies and heightening pleasures.

Inanna slipped back into the lights, which corresponded to her erotic sensations as they danced in the top of her head. Jehran studied her body as he kissed and caressed it. She was so very beautiful. Her breasts were small but full; her slim waist invited him to follow its lines down into her soft, smooth belly and her feminine curving thighs, which were various tones of creamy and inviting warm blues. Mmmm, he adored her, body and soul.

Jehran thought she was the perfect woman for him. Her highly developed nervous system gave Inanna the ability to receive his knowledge and mastery of the arts of love. He knew just how to bring her to ecstasy. One day soon he would, through this mastery, take her home with him into a higher reality. Jehran had dreamed of experiencing a dimensional shift with a highly evolved, responsive woman whom he greatly loved. Now it was the wonderfully deep and profound love that existed between Jehran and Inanna that would allow this experience to take place.

Jehran ceased moving his hands over her and gently pulled himself on top of her. Even though his phallus was perfectly erect, he did not enter her. Instead he focused his thoughts on being inside of her. Inanna felt him enter her, but knew that he had not done so physically; he was using the union of their considerable energies to move both of them up into a higher frequency. Jehran stretched himself out over her and as he melted into her, their energies began to entwine and merge on a level that transcended the physical. Like the symbol of Infinity itself, the reclining eight, their magnetic polarities wrapped themselves over and around each other on ever-deepening levels. As the two lovers flowed into one another, Inanna felt it would never end.

Far away in the forever Void, Thel Dar felt Inanna's energies expanding exponentially. The great radiant-light Being drew itself up into the form of a Torus, a ring of light rather like a golden doughnut shape of photons rolling into and over itself. As the ever-expanding energies of the loving couple increased, so did the rolling motion of Thel Dar's Torus; and in turn, the Torus itself began to spin the harmonies of their love out into all-the-possible worlds.

Back on Earth, Gracie felt herself to be in synchronicity, in a state of heightened awareness, as she continued playing Wolfie's music. Olnwynn sensed a wave of bliss move right through him, and he started laughing. In that exact moment, all of Inanna's multidimensional selves and Thel Dar's thought-projected beings found themselves magically lifted and expanded.

As Inanna and Jehran came to their completion, a surge of uplifting rapture rang out across the Universe. All-the-possible worlds were washed in the ecstasy of these lovers.

Wolfie lifted his consciousness out of Gracie's body as the last note faded from her piano. Gracie sighed deeply and said, "That was so beautiful. Never in my wildest dreams could I ever have imagined such an experience. You play the andante in a way I have never before heard it. It is obvious that the very tempo of life has changed since you were in a body of your own."

"Gracie!" Wolfie exclaimed. "I want to see life as it is now. I want to walk around with you on the streets of this place and just see things for myself. Will you accompany me?"

"I'd love to. You are one of my favorite people in all of history. Come on, let's go downtown and see the sights." Gracie threw on a raincoat and headed for the door with her friendly ghost. Wolfie floated into Gracie's pickup truck and the two trundled off the see the twentieth century in all its electrified glory.

Wolfie had a huge enthusiasm for almost anything and everything. He kept wanting to stop and look, all the while asking Gracie a gazillion questions. It was a good thing that Gracie was more than mildly infatuated with Wolfie; he would have worn out a less impassioned tour guide.

The two passed by a man lying on the sidewalk; the man was very dirty and obviously drunk. His hair was long and greasy, his clothes tattered, his hands practically black with city dirt. But his body was lean, still muscular from what must have been an active physical life. In fact, this man was a Northwest woodsman who had come to the city because he could find no work cutting down trees.

Ed, or Edward Paul Ross as he had been christened, came from a long line of woodsmen who took pride in know- ing the forests and in cutting the timber that was theirs for

71

the taking for three generations. The new laws which protected the environment had, unfortunately for Ed, made finding work impossible. His wife had tragically died in childbirth and the child had been lost along with her. Ed had wandered aimlessly from one small town to the next until he drifted into the big city. He drank excessively when he could afford it, and picked fights with other desperate men. Today he was at the end of his rope and had passed out on the sidewalk in front of a mission for lost souls. The concrete streets did not smell of sweet cedar or fresh mountain streams.

The sight of Ed sprawled out cold gave Wolfie a great idea. He called up Ed's spirit and began to negotiate. Wolfie wanted to "borrow" Ed's body for awhile. He promised to take excellent care of it. He just wanted to experience a few things in this third dimensional plane of polarities, a few earthly things—like the five senses.

Ed's spirit was impressed; Wolfgang Amadeus Mozart wanted to borrow his body? He had heard Wolfie's music occasionally through time in various incarnations; and it was becoming obvious that Edward Paul Ross was a mess. Even his body was beginning to deteriorate. His spirit was fed up with Ed's antics lately and had actually, just then, been thinking of giving up on Ed, getting a new body, and going somewhere else—maybe to Hong Kong, where there might be some fun times for him.

The two spirits struck a deal: Wolfie could "walk in" to Ed's body and keep it for as long as he wanted. When Wolfie was ready to leave, Ed's spirit had the option of returning or not. From the look of things, Wolfie felt certain that Ed's spirit had experienced more than enough from the DNA of this particular data-collecting vehicle. The two beings shook their etheric hands and the exchange was made.

Suddenly, much to Gracie's amazement, Ed's eyes began to shine brightly; the light of the genius of Wolfgang Amadeus Mozart was emanating from them. Ed's spirit waved good-bye as Wolfie lifted Ed's intensely soiled, odoriferous body from the sidewalk in front of the mission.

"Gracie, I need a bath."

Gracie held her nose. "Boy, you're not kidding!"

Wolfie noticed a minister standing in the mission doorway and called to him. "Sir, may I use your establishment to tidy myself up a bit?"

The minister was astonished; he had been trying to get Ed to shower for days, to no avail.

"Why sure, Ed! Help yourself. You know where everything is."

Wolfie stayed in the shower for almost an hour. He just couldn't get over how good it felt to have warm water spray out of the showerhead all over his body; well, once he got the stench off. Cleaning his hands was more difficult; his nails were encrusted with black tar. But Wolfie did his best. He washed what was now his long greasy hair; and as he dried himself off, he pulled his hair back into a ponytail and stared at his clothes. *This won't do,* he thought. Throwing the stinky, worn shirt and jeans on anyway, he went out to find Gracie.

"I believe I need some clothes. Look at these things."

Gracie knew just what to do; her mother, a shopaholic, had taught her well. She headed straight for a local men's clothing store, a place worthy of Herr Mozart.

As they entered the shop, Gracie flashed a credit card before the sales staff could throw Wolfie out.

"We need something Italian," she said haughtily. "Something tailored, I think, and your finest silk shirts. I trust you have a good selection of shoes."

The salesman smiled—what the hell, money was money —and brought out a selection of the latest in Italian suits.

Wolfie was delighted; he was a big overgrown child in every way, and the world was his to *play* in. He began to talk about the Italian tailors of his time. "Well, Bruno was my favorite. When Father and I had money, we would always order Signor Bruno's fine suits, cut from exquisite blue and white Chinese silks and, of course, trimmed with Belgian lace. All of Viennese society wanted Bruno's superb tailoring."

The salesman was perplexed; lace on a suit? Oh, well. So many new people had moved to the Pacific Northwest these days that he never knew who might come into the store. Maybe this fellow was from California, or maybe he was a rock star; but then, why did he look like a lumberjack?

Gracie paid the man and walked out of the store with Wolfie on her arm, his new and freshly showered body dressed in a classy Italian suit. As they walked toward the new grand adventures of the twenty-first century, they both thought: *Life is full of pleasant surprises, and timelessness has its advantages.*

X

THE BAND

Clarissa slept peacefully in Michael's arms. The two had made love until a sweet exhaustion came over them. Soundly asleep in their warm bed in the Pacific Northwest, Clarissa and Michael had, in their consciousness, joined Inanna and Jehran, Gracie and Wolfie, Olnwynn, and many others in another dimension.

Thel Dar was addressing them.

"I am. I am, in the mind of Prime Creator, one of many portions of the Creator's thought. I am a probability expressed as energy, manifesting Prime Creator's unlimited possibilities.

"Time does not exist; it is a useful illusion, a matrix through which thought projects the infinite varieties of dimensional frequencies.

"I, Thel Dar, project a part of myself as a multitude of beings of varying frequencies into all-the-possible worlds. I am Inanna, I am Gracie, I am Olnwynn, and many, many others. Some are forms not familiar to you; but all are important to me. I find beauty and wisdom in all life forms. They are all loved by me as portions of my *Self*, and thus as part of Prime Creator.

"When Gracie, for example, passes from this plane of existence—or, as you would say, dies—she will return to me. But for a time she will process the wisdom of her experiences with others of like frequency, and thus bring her knowledge and life data back into me. As the illusion of our separation ceases, Gracie will merge with me; in rejoining me she will expand herself, while retaining her separate identity. She will become me, and she will remain herself.

"The distances of space which serve to separate us do not exist unless measured by a frequency of time; Gracie will simply be, as I, Thel Dar, am.

"I am. I am Being, now and forever in the Mind of Prime Creator.

"Reincarnation, as you call it, does not take place in any linear manner. All things exist in the now; linear time is an illusion. I am eternally projecting parts of myself into all-the-possible worlds. Any of my multidimensional selves can have access to the others and to me, if they will only realize it by simply *knowing* they can. The past and the future can be easily accessed, because there is only the present.

"The human beings living in the time frequency on the surface of the planet Earth have forgotten their ability to expand beyond the limited frequencies they blindly accept. Their present reality is a very narrow band of frequencies which primarily defines the polarities of survival and fear. "There is much more of life to be lived."

The sunlight moved onto Clarissa's face as she lay in the bed. She opened her eyes and tried to remember her dream. The clock on her table told her it was noon. Like a happy cat, Clarissa stretched her beautiful young body and yawned contentedly. Her man was home.

Deep in outer space, Jehran wrapped his arms around Inanna and hugged her affectionately. "My darling, we are coming to the planet Valthezon now. We must dress to meet the dignitaries who will soon greet us and escort us to Central Pavilions."

Inanna yawned and snuggled deeper into her lover's warmth. "Must we, Jehran? It is so blissful here in your arms."

Jehran laughed softly and kissed her pretty blue nose. "Yes, my love, we must. I can feel my friends approaching the ship now."

Jehran had spent many years on the planet Valthezon, studying its systems of trade and economics. He had been sent there by his own planetary group as an observer and advisor. Valthezon, in addition to being the largest purveyor of the cocoa bean in this sector of the Universe, had also developed an interesting economic system based on trusting the value of something no one had ever even seen physically.

This large planet was covered with majestic mountains; seven of these mountains were noticeably higher than any of the others and served as the geographic center for each region or state. Each region had its own central mountain and was named after that mountain. The planet's inhabitants never warred region against region; they had passed that phase eons ago. But they did engage in competition. Each region vied with the others to produce the finest cocoa beans, and yearly contests were held to judge whose chocolatiers produced the finest chocolates.

The wealth of each region was based on the tradition that a magic stone lay concealed within each of the Seven Mountains. These magic stones, called the Qwoose, had the power to receive and transmit harmony and well-being among any and all people who would open themselves to such frequencies. The planet's archives revealed countless varied descriptions of each of the seven magic stones, and every region felt connected with the stone contained in its mountain.

No one on Valthezon had ever actually seen any of the Qwoose; they were known to be buried so deeply within each of the Seven Mountains as to be beyond reach. However, through the process of remote viewing, many respected and honored seers regularly observed the treasured stones embedded within the Seven Mountains. Thus the wealth of each region was based on the current visionary description of its Qwoose, and each region chose to trust such descriptions implicitly, without reservation.

Sometimes a new vision would provide a fresh description of a region's stone. A venerable seer would declare the indisputable enhancement of a stone to be the consequence of the local people having infused new energies into the mountain. This increase would be accepted as truth. Qualities such as trust, kindness, generosity, and, of course, love were said to increase the size and beauty of each magic stone, and thus the wealth of any particular region. It was a wonderful arrangement that had operated splendidly for generations, to the contentment of all Valthezon.

XI

FILM

Even though it was lunchtime and Clarissa was more than a little hungry, she decided to let Michael continue sleeping. Who knew what time it was in Peru, and those long plane rides were always so debilitating. Being careful not to wake him, Clarissa lay back into her pillows and closed her eyes again.

As she began to drift in the shadows and light behind her eyelids, she found that she could observe two simultaneous realities. It was as if two transparent movies were playing in the Eye of her Mind, like film laid over film, and she could choose to focus her consciousness on either one or both of them. But one was decidedly more pleasant than the other.

In one reality, Clarissa found herself as a three-year-old girl on board a very big spaceship. She was sitting on Gracie's lap; Gracie was singing funny songs to Clarissa and making her laugh. There was a sweet feeling of love between the two, as if they had long been friends in other times and places. Even though Clarissa's body was still adorably small, her consciousness was most certainly not; she knew intuitively who the great Beings were who had gathered here on what they called the Mother Ship.

In the other reality, Clarissa found herself in a hot, humid climate, dressed in cool white robes. Many other young women—priestesses of a great goddess of love— were there with her. Their sacred temple had been over- whelmed by a terrible army of reptile-like warriors. The priestesses had been ordered to worship the lord of these armies and to publicly deny their own beloved goddess. They had all adamantly refused, preferring to die rather than worship this odious tyrant warlord; they would never give up their love for the goddess.

Clarissa, the youngest and most beautiful, had been singled out as an example to the others. As the lizard men dragged her forward, their talons dug deep into her graceful white arms and her sweet red blood began to flow.

Once again, the movie vision split itself; now there were three scenes. In one, manacles and chains were placed on Clarissa's delicate ankles. She was thrown into the river and pulled thrashing by the soldiers, until a crocodile lifted its enormous head and swiftly ripped her left arm from her body. Their intentions complete, the vile men pulled her bloody, dismembered form from the waters to serve as a cruel warning to the others.

In another reality, the soldiers ripped her delicate arm right out of her body with their massive claws and began to chew on it, fighting over it. Both versions seemed equally real, vivid, and horrible to Clarissa.

Once again, she focused her consciousness back on the Mother Ship, and saw herself in the arms of Gracie, who was still laughing and kissing Clarissa's rosy baby cheeks. Two large silver doors opened slowly and two beautiful ladies entered the room. One woman had perfect ivory skin and long copper-red hair; her dress was covered in deep-red garnets. The other wore flowing silks of gold and silver; her skin was a warm turquoise blue. Both women were statuesque and looked like goddesses to Clarissa.

The blue lady spoke to Gracie. "Does Clarissa remember everything in the plan?"

"Yes, Inanna. While she is here on the ship, she remembers everything. She knows she must take on the veil of forgetfulness when she returns to her Earth home, but her time of awakening will correspond perfectly to the others'. All will join in remembering and waking up," Gracie answered joyfully.

"Good. Then let us go and meet with the others in the Great Hall." Inanna and the Lady of the Garnets walked toward the door arm in arm as old friends often do.

Gracie followed them into another part of the ship, carrying little Clarissa in her arms. There in a large room with silver walls and a well-lit vaulted ceiling, an assembly of diverse beings had gathered. There were many children here; some were of the human race and others were quite different. But all shared a collective purpose, and a sense of oneness and love.

As the energy in the room filled Clarissa, it uplifted her soul and found its way back to the bed where she lay with Michael. On the Mother Ship there was also a little boy who had to be Michael. He was making faces at little Clarissa, and she laughed and giggled because he was so funny.

Gracie was laughing too when five very grand and handsome beings entered the Hall. Anu and Antu, a couple who were husband and wife as well as brother and sister, came in.

Anu was tall, stately, and handsome; the hardships of exile had only served to refine his exquisite character. His lovely sister/wife, Antu, was the very soul of feminine beauty and sensuality. Antu had the face of a goddess, and the intelligence and wit of a great politician.

With them were the three children of Anu. Enlil's golden waves of hair were beginning to gray ever so slightly, but his body appeared strong and vigorous as ever. Next to Enlil stood his sister, Ninhursag; her pristine beauty was heightened by her obvious intelligence. Next to Ninhursag stood the second brother, Enki, who rather resembled Merlin the Magician and whose eyes twinkled softly, exuding a love for all life.

Everyone in the Great Hall focused on these five members of the family of Anu. Anu began the proceedings by introducing his daughter Ninhursag. She discussed the creation and genetic history of the species now living on planet Earth. Members of the audience expressed keen interest in precisely whose DNA the Earth humans possessed. Those who had contributed to the human genome felt that they had the right to continue breeding with the humans. After all, they were genetically a part of the human species, and thus claimed the right to participate in the program of genetic experimentation currently taking place with the earthlings.

Clarissa's child-mind kept wandering as she tried to

listen to Ninhursag; she felt she already knew this DNA stuff. She wanted to play with that funny little boy, and with those little Grey children with the big black eyes. Clarissa sensed that these gentle creatures were her friends.

From her bed in the Pacific Northwest where she was still lying comfortably, Clarissa looked up. Well, not really up, but rather *through* one film of reality into another. Thel Dar and many other radiant-light Beings in the forever Void were apparently watching Anu as he began to speak to those gathered on the Mother Ship.

Clarissa knew she was in her cozy bed with Michael as her present Earth self, while she was also a small girl sitting with everyone on the Mother Ship. She was simultaneously aware of her life as a temple priestess ravaged by the lizard soldiers. Realities overlay each other and flowed into each other. Realities existed separately; and yet, they were contained within each other like transparent film that vibrated in varying spheres of time frequencies. It was amazing!

Michael began to stir. Clarissa got out of bed and slipped into the kitchen to make him the most awesome breakfast he would ever eat. She felt fantastic, and it was time to celebrate!

XII

THE TRANSFORMATION

After a long day of meetings and conferences, Jehran and Inanna returned to their living quarters. Jehran knew the time had come for him to prepare Inanna for the transition into his home dimension. As they entered their guest suite, Jehran turned to his beloved and spoke softly.

"Inanna, the time has come."

From the sound of his voice, Inanna understood what he meant, and suddenly she felt a little unsure of herself. She was about to enter a world unknown to her, with only Jehran to guide her. Instinctively she nestled into his arms, waiting to feel his caress. But that was not to be.

Jehran sat Inanna on one side of the room on a soft pillow alone, and walked a distance away from her. Bewildered, Inanna watched him sit down and remove all his garments. He invited her to do the same. *But we are so far apart,* she thought.

Focusing his brilliant dark eyes upon her, Jehran began to generate a force field. In that moment, Inanna's uncertainty melted away, and she understood exactly what she must do. She looked deeply into the eyes of her beloved. He was the one man whose energies truly resonated with, and even equaled, her own. Jehran was and had always been that part of her that remained a mystery, that unknown elusive something she had continually sought in all of her lovers and all of her adventures. He was the expression of her secret self, and she longed to merge with him, to experience the totality of her being, now and forever.

Inanna carefully focused all of her thoughts on the energy centers in her body. In the Eye of her Mind, she saw the centers of creative and sexual energy as spheres of light and fire. She began to spin them with a concentrated intent of thought. The spheres in her lower body began to spin in an ever-increasing fervor. This in turn sent energy up Inanna's spine into the higher centers of her heart, throat, mind, and beyond. These spheres likewise increased their spin in response, and every receptor in Inanna's body was soon opened. Her consciousness combined with fiery spirit, and exponentially expanded her capacity to receive the Waters of Life—the essential energy.

Inanna looked across the room at Jehran.

He spoke. "You see, my love, there is no need for us to touch."

Jehran had been right about Inanna; she was the woman he had waited for.

And so, like a great symphony, a grand passionate play of energies moved back and forth across the room between these two. When one of them drew up more of the life force, it would expand and flow over into the other, building with each motion, each touch, each caress of thought. Their bodies became a fiery conduit for the Waters of Life, and thus began to change, to mutate, and to grow.

From Thel Dar's view, that room contained two white-hot lights spraying myriad blue and gold photons as a river of light, flowing in graceful waves across the room from one body and back into the other. As the tides of their ecstasy ebbed and flowed, their bodies did not appear to be solid, but rather were fluid—a liquid light that delighted in constantly transforming itself into incomparable patterns.

Jehran spoke into the heart of his beloved. "Do you still desire to follow me into my homeland? It will be a new adventure for you, Inanna, and it will require some adjustment on your part. You have free will, and now is the time for you to decide. Should you choose to accompany me, the Inanna you were will be expanded and will never again be quite the same."

Inanna laughed, thinking, *Oh, this is a great time for him to ask!* In all her life, she had never experienced such bliss—and Jehran had not even touched her. Only their eyes were locked in union through focus. His gentleness overwhelmed her, and yet, she never felt stronger. *I would follow this irresistible man to the far ends of the Universe,* she thought.

Jehran replied into her mind, "Well, yes, that is where we are going; but not this Universe. We will move outside the envelope of this Universe into another dimensional world altogether, a hyper-dimension. Ah, Inanna, there are so many worlds, so many wonderful places in the Mind of God. Consciousness is infinite and eternal; it only waits for us to knock upon its door and enter. Come with me, my woman."

A fiery hand from a higher frequency reached out to

Inanna. Flames of photons flashed across the room and enveloped her in bliss. As every cell in her body began to mutate, Inanna became aware of *knowing*. Knowing came into her as surely as the fire of Jehran's love. Inanna's mind transcended all of its limitations as it returned to a remembered, familiar state. She had been this before; she had been here before; she had known all of this before. She was climbing, no, sailing back home, back into the Mind of God, through Jehran's love.

Around the two lovers, all-the-possible worlds appeared and disappeared like layers of transparent time to tell their stories and then vanish once again. Time rolled out before them, and thus, satisfied with itself, curled back into its Source. Suddenly all was darkness; there was no more white-hot light. There was only the forever—the endless nothingness of the forever Void, stretching out beyond all time.

Inanna and Jehran gazed around. In the eternal nothingness of the forever Void was a powerful peace, and the infinite potential of all-the-possible worlds. Inanna was filled with joy and happiness. Life was, after all, an awesome game. Prime Creator endlessly played hide-and-seek with all the varying parts of Itself. Prime Creator loved everything in Its creation equally. Prime Creator was Love, and loved to make Love.

Inanna and Jehran became aware of Thel Dar's presence in the forever Void. Inanna remembered how this radiant-light Being had come to her so long ago. Thel Dar rolled over and showered the two lovers with a spray of delicate light.

"Thel Dar," the ever-curious Inanna asked, "are Jehran and I one in you?"

"Sometimes. Not always," Thel Dar answered. "On

one level we are, all of us, one. At times I melt into Jehran's soul-self, the one known as Tathata. The frequencies of our expressions are very harmonic and we play well together. At other times Tathata, Jehran's soul-self, prefers to be off creating worlds that I choose to merely observe."

A beautiful radiant-light Being, neither male nor female, then separated itself magically from Thel Dar and stood before them. Jehran knew this Being well. After all, he had throughout his life cultivated his innate ability to allow Tathata's consciousness to express itself, now and then, through him. At other times, Jehran chose to operate more or less on his own. In a free-will Universe and the chaos of creation's possibilities, there is always a choice.

Thel Dar spoke. "Inanna, you are changed. I am now able to insert an expanded consciousness into you. We will thus continue to unfold our realities together as we move through the dimensional universes.

"I love you, Inanna; I always have. You are so precious to me. Go and play; perhaps you and Jehran will make babies together. Tathata and I are looking for some enhanced data-collecting vehicles, what you call children, for us to express ourselves in. Go, beloved woman, and be happy."

In a nanosecond, Inanna found herself back in their room on the planet Valthezon, where Jehran was tenderly taking her in his arms. Tears of joy ran down Inanna's cheeks, and Jehran kissed them away. Inanna was happy and fulfilled. There was so much life ahead for both of them to cherish, just living every blessed moment knowing they were held in the eternal Love of God.

Jehran whispered softly to his beloved Inanna, "And so, my darling, now we are ready to travel!"

XIII

DINNER AND DEATH

As Wolfie, in his new body, walked into Gracie's house, the dogs jumped up with curiosity and excitement. Even showered, Ed Ross's body retained remnant odors interesting to canines. Gracie laughed as her big dog, Bear, who weighed 120 pounds, affectionately licked Wolfie's new face.

"Hey, Gracie! Are you sure this beast likes me?" Wolfie asked sincerely.

"My Bear loves everything and everyone," Gracie replied confidently.

Olnwynn, just waking up from a nap, was surprised to see Wolfie in a new body.

"Zounds! Where did you get *that?*" he asked.

Gracie and Wolfie explained that Ed Ross's spirit had agreed to let Wolfie borrow Ed's somewhat neglected body.

Hmmm, Olnwynn thought. *Well, look what can go on. Body-hopping. I, myself, am not quite ready to get back into another body. Personally, I think taking a break from the five senses would do me a lot of good right now.*

Olnwynn was anxious for a return visit to his pretty wife, who was now living in the form of Diana. He liked riding around with her in that enormous hulk of metal she called an automobile.

Wolfie and Gracie went into the kitchen; Wolfie couldn't wait to taste real food again after so many years. The two had stopped at a grocery store and brought home four bags stuffed with foods Wolfie wanted to eat. There were also two bottles of French wine, which Wolfie lost no time in opening.

Olnwynn decided to leave the two alone; there was no way he could join this third dimensional feast. Besides, he had a feeling this cozy kitchen scene might turn mushy —Gracie had that smitten-female look in her eyes. So Olnwynn bade his two friends farewell and again projected his consciousness into the back seat of Diana's luxury sedan.

In her kitchen, Gracie laid out all the exotic edibles Wolfie had insisted on buying. She tossed a Vienna sausage into Bear's mouth and held out another for the smaller female. Between sips of wine, Wolfie shoved samples of everything into his own mouth and simultaneously fed the dogs. It was a stand-up banquet for all.

At last, they could eat no more. Gracie and Wolfie took their glasses of wine into the living room and sank down together into the deep, comfortable couch.

"Wolfie," Gracie asked, "Why did you drink so much when you were alive?"

"I was lonely."

"Lonely? How could that be? You were famous, you had your wife, and you had your music."

"I was desperately and utterly lonely. As a child I was the prodigy of the palace and the center of attention. Considered a genius, I was fawned over by aristocrats and kings. But a child does not know what a "prodigy" is; he only knows what he can do, and that he wants to be loved. My childhood was all performance and discipline. My father was my taskmaster, and I was completely dependent on his judgment. When it came to life and the people in it, I never developed the ability to make judgments for myself. Father did everything for me, and I never really grew up. When he died, it was too late for me to learn.

"The concerts were always followed by parties. I was gorged with cakes and wines, and indulged by all the pretty ladies of the court. It was cold in those great castles, and we were always drinking. As I grew older, the loneliness I felt deepened into constant pain. I felt an unbearable melancholy, which the drink temporarily eased."

"Oh, your heart was broken," Gracie said sadly.

"Yes," he continued. "I suppose you might call it a broken heart. I only knew that I hurt. I endured an unrelenting pain which eventually nothing could erase, not the wine, not the ladies, and ultimately—not even the music. There were times when the music would lift me above the pain. For a few sublime moments, I felt as if I were in another world, another realm, where everything was vaporous, vibrating light; and I felt myself to be at one with that light, no longer separate and alone.

"But then the music would end and I would find myself back in my body, with bills to pay, an unhappy wife, the memories of my childhood, and an overwhelming sense of helplessness. No one could help me, the great genius and child prodigy.

"I had enemies, of course, at the court. Men who were jealous of my genius, and naturally the women I had loved and betrayed. So I drank and I gambled compulsively, losing everything. I kept borrowing more money, kept gambling and losing.

"Then I became very ill. I struggled with my illness for a long time. As we became destitute, my wife was possessed with fear, and angry with me for failing her.

"Finally I died. I remember so well watching two chaps unceremoniously dump my body into a pauper's grave, right on top of other decaying bodies. They sprinkled lime over me to hasten the decomposition process. What a shock! What an ugly sight for me! I moved on rather quickly after that. It wasn't as though there were hundreds of grieving friends mourning my death. Everyone, except my creditors, seemed to have forgotten the great Mozart, the prodigal genius. I thought, *Where are they now? How could they forget me so soon?*

"My wife was so overcome with despair that she came close to destroying all of my music. In death, I had abandoned her with nothing save my gambling debts. She wanted revenge. She wanted to hurt me, even though I was already dead and beyond her vengeance.

"After the funeral, my wife Constanze sat in our shabby flat alone drinking glass after glass of the cheap wine I had kept hidden around the place. Mesmerized by the small crackling fire before her, the anger she felt toward me burned into her very soul. She hated me.

"Suddenly she moved to my writing desk and hastily grabbed up piles of sheet music. I panicked; surely she wasn't going to burn my music. My spirit cried out to her; she was determined, and it took all of my energy to stop her. She dropped to the floor in a sobbing heap, holding my music in her arms.

"I can remember the early times, when she first loved me; how she could laugh. I was the center of her world then."

Gracie sighed. Even for a creative genius, a prodigy, life could be hard and hurt so much.

"Then what happened?" she asked.

"I felt myself being pulled by a powerful force, as if by a magnet," Wolfie continued. "Suddenly, there was a radiant-light Being, who called itself Tathata, standing in front of me—a Being who said it *was* me. I couldn't imagine myself, certainly not at that moment, to be so incredibly perfect, so effulgent, so beautiful. After all, even though women had often found me irresistible, in my life I was a rather short man with a large nose.

"This perfect Being, Tathata, who claimed to be me, explained that I had been on a special mission to bring, through my music, a certain frequency into the third dimensional plane of planet Earth. Tathata had apparently volunteered to project a part of itself *as me* into Earth time, in order to create my unimaginably pure music, which was designed to lift the consciousness of every human who listened to it.

"Tathata said that because this is a free-will Universe, no one could predict what would happen once they found themselves in the lower frequencies of the third dimension. Not even the grandest of the radiant-light Beings ever knew exactly what to expect once they became locked in human bodies, whose DNA was more than mildly dysfunctional; and once in, they were trapped by the five senses in an environment of fear, disease, and endless wars.

"According to Tathata, I had on the one hand been successful. The music I had created would be played throughout the coming centuries, and would later be recorded by machines, as mankind developed new technologies.

"But, on the other hand, it seemed that I had fared rather less well in certain areas; and, as much as Tathata kept saying how much he/she/it loved me and regretted it, there remained certain things for me to resolve, lessons for me to learn, a completion of sorts for me to achieve. Tathata told me not to worry; there was nothing for me to be afraid of. This phase I was now entering was all part of a learning process, an exercise in self-mastery as it were, that we all go through. I had to do this on my own, pretty much without Tathata.

"Then Tathata told me that under no circumstances was I to let anyone touch me. This warning gave me a small chill. I was still struggling to rid my mind of the image of lime being tossed on my stiffening corpse.

"Tathata then led me into a long tunnel of light, and the next thing I saw was my father. I had mixed feelings about that. I loved my father dearly; but during his life he had always told me what to do, what not to do, what to play, and who to be nice to. I had gotten used to being on my own, so I was a little reticent when he began to tell me about this church where thousands upon thousands of righteous souls prayed continuously. He wanted me to join them and write music for them.

"As my father endeavored to embrace me, I remembered what the radiant-light Being, whom I had come to regard as my own soul, had said to me. *Don't allow anyone to touch you, Wolfie!* So I didn't. I backed away from my father's embrace, and ignored the perplexed, hurt look on his face. He entreated me with tales of the glories of the heavens; but somehow the whole scene just didn't feel right to me. Call me bad, but I didn't want to pray for all eternity. I was thinking it might be fun to do something besides music in a future life, like ride a motorcycle or drive a race car.

"So I rejected my father, refused to embrace him; and the more I denied him, the more he began to fade away.

"That wasn't the end of it, however; my mother promptly appeared to me and launched into a similar routine. Then came some of the more impressive members of the nobility I had known at court. I guess I was supposed to be easily intimidated by these men and women, who continued to plead with me. But apparently, unless I allowed it, they couldn't touch me; and the more I resisted them, the quicker they faded into a mist.

"I really didn't know what any of this meant, but I felt very good about it.

"Next I found myself in a room that was heavy with an overwhelming stench of stale brandy. The alcohol vapors saturated my consciousness. My old drinking and gambling buddies were all in that smelly room; their once-splendid silken clothing was stained and tattered. An excellent billiards table lay before us, and as we began to play, some of the louts I was indebted to began to press their claims.

"Once again I remembered not to touch them. I refused even a handshake. I found myself telling them, "You! You're not at all real!" And then, before my very eyes, these men I had once known, with whom I had shared many a bottle, turned into glistening, writhing snakes. Like the brandy vapors, they rose up into the air. My compulsion to gamble, and my incorrigible craving for alcohol, vanished like their spirits.

"I had once belonged to the Freemasons, and I had acquired some secret knowledge in my life, but nothing could have prepared me for this.

"Surrounded by infinite blackness, I began to feel lonely again. I began going over the events of my short life, recalling every ecstatic and wretched detail. What a life I had lived! I thought of all the delicious women I had seduced; I remembered their lace gowns, their soft, supple breasts, and their honey-red lips.

"Then, in that vast darkness, I heard my sublime music. I remembered myself composing; in life, I could barely write fast enough to get the notes on paper. The music had coursed through me like a torrential river.

"Truly, I never wanted to write down my music; but it was the only way to get money, which I loved to spend. I preferred to improvise each time I sat in front of the harpsichord or piano. I heard the music in my heart; I felt it in my soul. Music was always there for me, and as I created, I let each note slip into the silence of eternity.

"Why would anyone want to play the same piece over and over? Wouldn't everyone want to play his or her own music? I grasped that the humans had tragically lost their ability to hear the music within their souls. My music was needed for the uplifting of the human race.

"Observing my wildly exuberant and creative life only increased my loneliness. Here I was all alone, somewhere out in Eternity.

"Then Tathata reappeared, radiant as ever, and said to me, "Well done, Master Amadeus, he whom God loves!"

"At that moment a grand piano, perfect beyond my wildest dreams, materialized for me. I sat down to play. My concertos, symphonies, and sonatas spilled out across the universes into all-the-possible worlds within the Mind of God.

"As I played, my entire being began to resonate at higher and higher vibrational frequencies. I became one with the sounds I played, and I *knew* who I was. I remembered that I had gone into the third dimension to perform a task. I had been on a mission to serve Prime Creator, to generate sounds that would lift the hearts and minds of men, to help free them from the endless confusion of fear. My music had created a safe harbor of purity and innocence on the planet Earth, by reflecting the Love that flows from the Mind of God and generates all Life. I had fulfilled my task.

"And so, rapt in the experience of remembering my Oneness with all Life, I remained there playing until you and Olnwynn happened to pass by with your friends Clarissa and the lady Inanna."

Gracie leaned over and kissed Wolfie; he took her in his arms. Holding someone close felt good to him. Wolfie's new body, the body of Edward Paul Ross, felt the healing warmth and tenderness of love for a woman slowly gathering force within him. And so, this unlikely couple sat cozily on a sofa in the Pacific Northwest with two dogs curled up at their feet. Holding each other for a very long time, they both fell into a deep and profound sleep.

XIV

SHOPPING AND VANISHING

Olnwynn admired the rich leather seats in Diana's luxury sedan. He had of course never seen such things in second-century Ireland. Just by looking at it, he knew the leather was very soft; he wished he could touch it. He wished he could touch Diana. Where was she?

His reveries were interrupted.

"She's not here." Olnwynn's brother from ancient Ireland, Diana's now-deceased and most recent husband, Brent, floated outside the car with his head stuck through the windshield. "She's gone."

"Where did she go?" Olnwynn asked.

"She's in a hospital with a lot of other old people, mostly women. She's sort of there, and not there—I guess you could say she's not all there, or not there all the time."

"What are you talking about, my brother?" Olnwynn was getting confused.

"Come on. I'll show you. You can see for yourself." Brent motioned for Olnwynn to follow him, and the two men soon found themselves in a small hospital ward. Seven beds lined each side of the room; the beds were occupied by elderly ladies in varying states of consciousness. They all had long transparent tubes stuck in their arms, and liquids dripped through those tubes into their lethargic, spiritless bodies. It seemed to Olnwynn that they were drugged (not that he knew much about drugs; he had always preferred alcohol). As a child, he had been placed in the care of the Druids, and he had watched the priests drink liquid concoctions of crushed red and white mushroom caps. The priests then had visions and talked to fairy folk. During such rituals, Olnwynn would go off hunting. He saw the priests' ceremonial inebriations as a chance to escape his chores.

But this was very different. Olnwynn had the distinct sense that these women were purposely being sedated, whereas the priests had made a choice.

"They just want 'em quiet so they don't cause anybody any trouble," Brent said angrily in his Southern drawl. "If I were still alive I'd have my Diana out of this place so fast it would make your head spin."

"Oh." Olnwynn felt out of sorts. He was bewildered by this place. He hated seeing Diana hooked up to tubes and bottles. She was so pale, and her arms were bruised from needle marks.

Then, as if from nowhere, she, or rather her spirit's consciousness, showed up.

"Hi there, you two! My, it's nice to have two husbands.

I mean two beaus." Her physical body was still lying comatose, flat on the bed. But here she was, apparently floating above it, right in front of them.

"Are you dead?" Olnwynn asked her.

"No, I don't think so. I was so darned bored in this place that I taught myself to get out of this old body. I think it's called astral traveling, or something like that— but wouldn't that mean traveling with the stars?" Diana was flushed with excitement.

"Where have you been, Dear?" Brent asked.

"Shopping! Now I can spend all the time I want to in the couture sections of the big department stores. Everyone's doing it. Come on, I'll show you." Diana waved her menfolk onward to housewife heaven.

Neither Brent nor Olnwynn had the slightest interest in couture *anything*. Brent had always detested shopping; it just wasn't manly. And Olnwynn didn't really know what shopping *was*. But Diana said everyone was doing it, and that had made them both curious.

Soon the three found themselves in one of those big glitzy shopping malls, in a very fancy department store, in the section that sold high-priced designer clothes. Several middle-aged women wearing fur coats and diamond rings wandered around looking for expensive clothing to restore their fading charms. There were a few elderly matriarchs, and also some younger women who were going through the sales rack.

Brent looked at the price tags, remembering Diana's clothes bills. *Who the hell can afford these damned clothes*, he thought. *What a racket!*

Floating among the live customers were many more not-so-live customers. Giving a new meaning to "shop 'til you drop," these disembodied spirits of older and ill women had learned to escape the confines of their declining days and were now thoroughly enjoying themselves at their favorite department store.

Olnwynn quickly grew bored. He thought of moving on to a department called "Outdoor and Sports" he had noticed near the entrance. Then he remembered Diana's predicament. He had always wanted to make up for the way he had treated her in Ireland. In those days, he had been consistently unfaithful to her, and he had struck her more than once. Even when she had behaved like a shrew, she hadn't deserve such abuse. *There must be a way to rescue her from that awful place,* he thought. Surely, not even Diana would want to shop for all eternity.

"Diana, don't you want us to get you out of that hospital ward?"

Diana was deep in the cocktail dresses and making her way to the evening gowns. "Well, of course, Olnwynn. But how?"

Deep in space, Jehran gave the final orders for the preparation of his ship and its occupants for a more subtle dimension. He knew that Inanna was now ready to make the journey with him; every cell in her body, every strand of her DNA, had mutated perfectly; she would be able to withstand the higher-dimensional frequencies they were about to enter into.

Each body in every dimension is normally designed to accommodate only its "home" dimension, meaning the dimension of its origin. Inanna came from a race which had originally evolved in the Pleiades; the DNA of her great-grandfather, Anu, and her great-grandmother, Antu, had been handed down to her through her grandparents, Enlil and Ninlil, and her parents Nannar and Ningal. Her body's genetic code met the demands of the worlds she was born to inhabit. Jehran's world, as he had explained to her, was remarkably different.

For one thing, there were no tyrants in his dimension. Everyone who lived in Jehran's world had evolved past the level of needing to control others. After living through the destruction wrought by the tyrants of Nibiru and Earth—especially by her reptilian cousin Marduk—a world that had outgrown tyranny sounded perfectly refreshing to Inanna.

Jehran explained, however, that the biggest problem his world faced was an innocuous form of boredom. People in his dimension occasionally opted to leave their perfect, non-polarized world and pop right back down into some struggling tyrannical frequency. They actually wanted to experience living in a body with five limiting senses. They saw the big challenges, like survival and forgetting who they were, as fun. After all, the free-will universes *did* exist for a reason, and Prime Creator kept all-the-possible worlds going as long as there was a demand for them.

Inanna tried to imagine Earth without tyrants. She knew it was up to the people who inhabited planet Earth to decide their future. It was simple: Their collective consciousness could create a world without controllers if they truly wanted it.

Jehran gave the command for the ship to be put into hyper-luminescence. Inanna stretched her imagination into the world he was taking her to. As she gazed out into deep space, she felt no gravitational pressure change. The entire ship they had been traveling on simply disappeared—vanished all around them, as it were. Inanna, a little disoriented, looked around for Jehran.

"Hold onto my consciousness, pretty lady. Don't look down! You will adjust to this soon."

Inanna saw her blue hands and body becoming translucent; even her jewelry was beginning to fade in a vaporous mist. Every material thing beneath and above them, including their bodies, dissolved into nothingness. Inanna and Jehran, along with everyone else on the entire magnificent ship, became pure thought. Their bodies, in all the infinite alien varieties onboard the ship, were gone.

Inanna felt free, and so light. She let go of Jehran for a moment and bounced around like a bubble. Intoxicated by her new freedom, she found she had no boundaries. There *were* no boundaries. There was no ship, and they had no bodies. They were moving through space as pure thought. Inanna giggled; losing control for a moment, she looked for Jehran. In his conscious thought, he reached out to anchor her.

"There, how is that, my darling?" Jehran asked.

"Wow! This is fantastic. I'm having so much fun!" Inanna was ebullient. *What a high!* she thought.

Jehran warned her, "You must focus just a little to stay with us. We are headed toward a particular destination. If you become distracted and allow your thoughts to wander, you might end up somewhere far away from us. In point of fact, you will end up wherever your focus is; and I want you with me."

"You say the best things, Jehran. Of course I will stay with you." Inanna concentrated her focus on this man whom she dearly loved. She knew that her mind still possessed a slightly unruly tendency to wander. She thought of her great-grandmother Antu's palace on Nibiru and the parties she had attended there as a child. Just as quickly as a thought came to her, she let it pass on out of her mind like a cloud crossing the sky.

A vision of the kingdom she had created on Earth came before her. Inanna saw magnificent cities of silver and lapis lazuli, and heard the melodious music flowing from her splendid Temples of Love. Her consciousness was flooded with memories of the past.

Inanna saw Sargon standing before her strong and handsome. Inanna had fallen in love with Sargon and made him King; together the two lovers had built a kingdom named Akkad and a shimmering city of love, Agade. They had enjoyed many years of happiness together until Sargon began to age; he had not been able to accept his own mortality in the face of Inanna's enduring youth and beauty.

Inanna lived within a duration of time separate from that of the humans; 3,600 human years equaled only one year for Inanna. Sargon was human; as his youthful strength and virility faded, he began to drink excessively. Inanna watched helplessly as the man she loved became belligerent and self-indulgent. In his hopeless confusion, Sargon offended the Lord Marduk, bringing famine and devastation to Akkad. Before he died, Sargon had cursed Inanna. The memory of seeing him on his deathbed trembling in sweat burned in her mind, even as the scenes of their early love-making remained etched in her heart. Sargon's death had forced Inanna to change.

Realizing that her emotional memories generated a magnetic field which pulled her into another reality, Inanna stopped the images cold. She did not want to return to the past, even though she had once loved Sargon. Inanna was now exactly where she wanted to be—with Jehran.

Whoops! Inanna blushed. Jehran could always read her thoughts and now *nothing* remained to mask them. She was an open book to this man who adored her in spite of, or perhaps even because of, her imaginative, lively, adventurous life.

"Yes, Inanna, I love you just as you are. We have even greater experiences to enjoy in this hyper-luminal state of being. When we make love, we will fuse our creative energies together as thought. We will be limited only by the boundaries we place upon our own thoughts. There is always so much more to experience. As easily as this"— Jehran paused to turn himself into a sphere of exquisite light—"we can become lights to dance and play among the stars. You will be pleased."

Inanna was pleased already. She carefully attached herself to Jehran's thoughts, his consciousness, and settled herself into the journey, which obviously was going to take a little time in a world where time does not exist.

Jehran tenderly embraced his beloved and looked out at the part of the Universe they were passing through to make sure they were on the proper course. He had set the coordinates to guide them all safely home. He had been away from his world for a very long time, and it would be good to be back. He was curious to see his old friends. He wondered who among them had chosen to pass on into new and different forms. Jehran wondered what would be waiting for him in the place he called home.

XV

SHIPS OF LIGHT

Gracie and Wolfie were awakened by the dogs' barking and a loud knocking at the front door.

"Gracie, it's me, Clarissa. Let us in."

Gracie opened her door to Clarissa and Michael.

"You won't believe what we just saw!"

Wolfie tried to introduce himself to Michael, but the excited Clarissa wasn't interested in anything except telling Gracie what she and Michael had just witnessed in a nearby park.

"Gracie, you've got to come and see them! Ships of light are coming down from the sky, everywhere—it's like we're being invaded or something! I couldn't believe my eyes!"

"Where did you see them?" Wolfie asked. The idea of seeing spaceships of light fly down to Earth was exciting.

Michael answered for the out-of-breath Clarissa.

"Man, it's incredible—just like the visions I had at Machu Picchu. These spaceships are hovering over the trees in the park. You want to see them?"

"Let's go," Wolfie answered.

Gracie was careful to leave the dogs in the house as she and Wolfie rushed out and followed Clarissa and Michael down the sidewalks for several blocks. The four stood in bewildered amazement at the sight of thirty or more disc-shaped vehicles hovering among the trees in the park. The discs were small in comparison to the Mother Ship. They emitted a glowing phosphorescent light that illuminated the night. A very subtle frequency of sound came from the ships—a soft, almost soothing, whirring.

Lots of people stood around in silence staring at the spaceships. Should they approach, or wait for someone or something to come out to them? No one knew what to do. They just stood there in silent wonder.

These days, people actually *wanted* alien ships to come to Earth—to show themselves. Everyone was tired of hearing the government, over and over, deny everything that anyone dared to report about UFO sightings. Recently, there had been a meeting at a major university to discuss alien abductions. But denial continued to be government policy. No one could figure out why, because almost everyone had either seen a UFO or had some kind of experience with the aliens, or at least knew someone who had. There was just too much evidence around to be ignored, even by the skeptics.

Gracie, Wolfie, Clarissa, and Michael just stood there with the others in the dark, wondering; not knowing whether to be frightened or glad, to run away or to stay put. They only wanted to know—what was the truth?

Fifteen or twenty minutes went by. Suddenly, as quickly as they had come, the ships of light took off and headed for the deep dark skies. The audience watched the ships disappear among the stars. They all lingered for a little while longer, and then quietly walked back to their homes. They knew that tomorrow the news would carry no reports of spaceships in the park. There might be a story about a fraternity prank or some other such nonsense.

But all of the gentle people who had gathered there that night knew what they had seen, and they would remember. All of them would be somehow changed because of that experience—being there in the park, standing together watching the ships of light, and listening to the soft whirring sounds. They would all be changed forever.

Gracie, Wolfie, Clarissa and Michael walked home in the dark.

Wolfie walked beside Michael, who recounted his experiences in Peru. Michael told of the ships he had seen landing at Machu Picchu thousands of years ago—the ships that had transported gold to an orbiting space station.

"I had a teacher at Machu Picchu," Michael said, "who called himself the Commander. He told me that I was some-how connected to the Pleiades through him."

Wolfie's consciousness was accessing some of the data in Ed Ross's body. It seemed that Ed had seen at least two UFOs. Late at night and deep in the woods where he had been logging, Ed had been taken onboard a ship by the Grey aliens with big black eyes. Wolfie thought that these aliens must not be so friendly; they treated Ed's body as if it were a kind of laboratory experiment. There was a scar on Ed's knee, perhaps from some invasive operation; and he had a sense that something sexual had occurred, although not exactly anything Wolfie would call fun.

Wolfie asked, "So, according to this Commander fellow, are there friendly aliens and some not so friendly?"

"Yes," Michael answered. "Apparently some of them have a real vested interest in our well-being, while others only want to manipulate us. Some are just here to observe us—to watch."

Gracie interrupted. "Yes, Inanna once explained it all to me. Long ago, a group of aliens colonized Earth and interfered with our natural evolution by actually tampering with our DNA. Apparently there is some ineluctable law in this Universe called the law of free will. Anyone who breaks that law will eventually reap the consequences of such acts; the negative effects will flow back into his or her reality, and that is exactly what is happening now.

"Some of the same beings who altered our genetics ages ago," Gracie continued, "are now back to help us wake up, to remember who and what we are. They have come to assist us to in reactivating our latent DNA. The human genome was partially unplugged, left dysfunctional; and that contributed to the sad, repetitive story of human history."

Wolfie, who was beginning to have a feeling for what Gracie was saying, joined in.

"After my death, when I remembered I had been sent to Earth to infuse her vibrational frequencies with my music, I also understood that I was part of a larger group of souls who were likewise inserting themselves throughout time in order to uplift the human spirit. We had all chosen to help the human race remember, as most beings in other universes remember, that everyone is a part of Prime Creator."

Each of the four friends, Gracie, Wolfie, Michael, and Clarissa, had an experience, a memory, to share with the others. It was as if each held a piece of a giant puzzle—and if all of the humans who were waking up could share their parts of the puzzle, all would benefit. None was more or less important than any other.

"Michael, what did you mean when you said they want to manipulate us?" Clarissa inquired.

"Well, if you're ready for this one, Honey: The Commander said something about a group that has learned to feed on our energies, our fears and anxieties. They manipulate this world in order to generate a continual supply of psychic energy for their consumption. The Commander calls them the gods of the Phantasmal Hierarchies. Apparently, they don't want to incarnate; they just stay in their own dimension and feed on our fear. The fact that we don't even know they exist makes it easy for them. They love wars and battlefields, stuff like that. It's hard to imagine."

At that, Gracie said, "I think we should all go back to my house and project our consciousness into Inanna's and Thel Dar's reality."

"Good idea," said Clarissa. "Let's go ask Thel Dar what's really going on."

"Who's Thel Dar?" asked Michael.

"You'll find out." Wolfie was catching on to some twentieth-century colloquialisms and rather enjoying himself. "Don't worry, man, you'll like it!"

XVI

PHANTASMAL HIERARCHIES

Motionless in the forever Void, Thel Dar contemplated all-the-possible worlds. Throughout the Mind of Prime Creator, *Is-ness* expressed itself as conscious thought projected into an infinite diversity of universes, each resonating at its own precise dimensional frequency.

Occasionally, a third dimensional world became entrapped. A 3-D world—for example, the planet Earth—could often be unpleasant, dangerous, and risky. The incarnating souls who were just too lazy to evolve themselves to a higher frequency often became weary of the perils of the lower frequencies. Once they were disincarnate and free of their vulnerable physical bodies, these wily entities learned to utilize the energies which were emitted from the physical and emotional bodies of those still stuck in 3-D time and space—and they cleverly used these "borrowed" energies to build vast hierarchical worlds.

Enlightened beings referred to the worlds of these errant soul groups as the Phantasmal Hierarchies. Thel Dar liked to call these gods "those lazy, loafing, good-for-nothing energy consumers!"

Knowing that Gracie, Clarissa, Michael, and Wolfie were about to call Inanna and request a visit to the forever Void, Thel Dar contemplated how to tactfully portray the intricacies of the Phantasmal Hierarchies. Even though this sort of thing happened all the time all over the galaxies, the current inhabitants of an entrapped world consistently found this sort of information troublesome and difficult to accept. Even Inanna didn't fully realize to what extent she and her family, the family of Anu, including the reptilian tyrant Marduk, had been a working part of the layers of the Phantasmal Hierarchies which surrounded the little blue and green sphere known as Earth.

Especially difficult was the part about the "apparent heavens." Deceased souls could plainly observe the tiers of heavenly worlds displayed before them, and those who thought they deserved hell could see those abysmal worlds. But what they could not realize was that all of those layered visions were merely holographic displays controlled by those who benefited from them. It was another form of limitation; as long as you thought you were in the ultimate place, you were stuck there. In fact, the souls who controlled these hierarchical worlds were getting a little bored. After eons of the same old thing, *any* heaven gets boring. A person/being wants to move on to do something else.

A self-selected few enlightened beings—like Thel Dar—who had created many of the existing universes had taken up a hobby. Going into these trapped worlds disguised as humans and breaking up "stuck" systems had become a favored adventure. It was great fun to shatter the endless maze-like traps of the Phantasmal Hierarchies—especially those set by the really pious, self-righteous, and pompous souls. Those who enjoyed tormenting their poor brothers and sisters needed to be lifted out of their confusion. When their worlds fell apart, hardened tyrants became constructively bewildered; propelled into a *remembering*, they could start to create a new reality. Thel Dar, and others of a similar disposition, offered those souls with a proclivity for tyranny a chance to move on and evolve.

Besides, Thel Dar thought, the inhabitants of the Phantasmal Hierarchies continually spoiled things for everyone else. Planet Earth had been entrapped now for far too long, imprisoned by illusions and by those lazy, good-for-nothing tyrants who wanted everyone else to do all the work.

But the question remained—how to tell Gracie and the others without throwing them into abject fear?

Dawn was just starting to glow as Gracie, Wolfie, Clarissa, and Michael sat down in Gracie's living room and began to focus their consciousness. The dogs lay quietly beside them, the house was still, and only a few birds could be heard singing their first morning notes in the garden. After seeing the ships of light, the four friends had no trouble in focusing.

Inanna and Jehran were still traveling as thought forms through space without a ship. Inanna had left a part of her consciousness in the Oval in the Snake Kingdom of Inner Earth so that Gracie could easily find her whenever she might need her.

"Jehran, Gracie is calling me," she said.

"Your present state as a thought form will not hinder your ability to manifest your lovely blue self to Gracie," he answered. "In fact, it will facilitate your mastery of the process in some ways. When you *have* no solid form, it is far easier to remember that there *are* no solid forms. All forms are merely thoughts manifesting themselves in varying frequencies as holograms. You will find it even easier now to project yourself into different realities, as you will no longer imagine you possess the limitations of any one form."

Inanna sighed. "That's nice."

"Come, a part of me will accompany you to the forever Void," Jehran said.

Inanna was happy to know Jehran would come with her. "But first we must stop off to pick up Gracie and her friends," she said. "They do not, as yet, imagine they can go without us."

In a nanosecond, Jehran and Inanna found themselves standing in their familiar bodies in the middle of Gracie's living room. Jehran was amazed to find one of his multidimensional selves there, but in a strange youthful body.

"Wolfgang Amadeus Mozart!" he exclaimed. "Where did you get that body?"

"Oh, my," Wolfie replied. "It's you!"

Wolfie hadn't seen Jehran in what seemed like ages, but now it was all coming back to him. Toward the end in Vienna, Jehran had often appeared to Wolfie and tried to help him when his life was sinking into debt and alcohol, when no one would commission him to write music. Jehran had been a friendly spirit to Mozart in those times. Wolfie, once he was dead, realized that Jehran had played an invaluable part in creating the Earth mission of the great composer Amadeus. Jehran was one of Tathata's multidimensional selves, just as Wolfie was.

"What a pleasure to see you, old man!" Jehran was truly delighted.

Inanna knew this was no mere coincidence. And she could tell immediately that something more than just friendship was going on between Gracie and this Wolfie character. Well, he *was* cute, and Gracie looked happier than Inanna had ever seen her. After all, both of them *knew* who they were. They had, individually, passed through the veil of forgetting and had remembered that they were a part of the eternal life force of Prime Creator. Inanna felt that perhaps Gracie and Wolfie were a good match, like Jehran and herself.

Wolfie excitedly related everything that had happened to him in the last two hundred years or so, as well as last night's witnessing of the ships of light. Clarissa and Michael sat patiently listening; they were getting used to all kinds of occurrences they might once have called miracles.

Noticing Clarissa and Michael, Inanna transmitted an invitation out to the Commander and his Lady of the

Garnets, her friend. Their prompt arrival elicited a celebration of reunions. After many hellos and embraces, there remained important questions to ask of Thel Dar. Still sitting in the Pacific Northwest, the members of the party projected themselves in thought to the forever Void and the abode of the radiant-light Being Thel Dar. Tathata was there also, which shouldn't have surprised anyone. It was a family meeting, a family of souls.

XVII

ANSWERS

The infinite blackness of the forever Void surrounded them all. There was no up and no down, no backward or forward, no beginning and no end. Thel Dar appeared to them as a magnificent, beautiful radiant-light Being. The unlimited *knowingness* and perfect harmonies of pure Love emanated from this gracious Being as golden cascading rainbows of phosphorescent photons.

Inanna began, feeling the others might find themselves a little tongue-tied by the majestic presence before them. "Thel Dar, we have come to ask you for answers."

"Yes, my beloved Inanna. I know your hearts and minds. I know why you have come. I have invited Tathata, my friend, to assist in enlightening you. Tathata is, of course, very familiar to Jehran and Herr Mozart.

"Your questions need only to form themselves to

magnetize their answers," Thel Dar explained. "It is the process of formulating the question that is most arduous for souls. Then they must be able to listen to the answer in order that they may hear. But that is another matter."

Michael, being young and impatient, blurted out, "Tell us about the ships of light we saw in the park." The whole question of UFOs had become an obsession with him ever since his abduction and the visions at Machu Picchu.

Thel Dar said, "The ships of light you witnessed are holographic thought-forms placed there by enlightened beings who desire to free the planet Earth from her entrapment. For far too long, Earth's inhabitants have been virtually imprisoned within repeating cycles which predominantly occur in a narrow band of frequencies known as the survival-and-fear polarities.

"The inhabitants of planet Earth, the human species, have been told for centuries that they are all alone in the entire Universe. This is absurd, naturally; and it has had the effect of increasing self-centered, small-minded, narcissistic attitudes which inevitably lead to prejudice, conflict, and war.

"If the humans living on planet Earth can understand, as they will very shortly, that an infinite number of other civilizations exist in the vastness of creation, they will evolve beyond their heliocentric narcissism and release their antagonistic tendencies. They will become, by necessity, more tolerant of other races.

"They will learn to value their Earth, now that they are coming perilously close to destroying it; they will discover how truly precious this little blue-and-green sphere is. Eventually, they will come to realize that Earth itself is a living being, a creating soul in and of itself."

Thel Dar paused, and looked to Tathata and Jehran for

support. Tathata took over.

"In the beginnings of life on the planet Earth," Tathata said, "some of the souls who were incarnating there quickly grew weary of the precarious nature of life in a third dimensional realm. The experience of being continually and unpleasantly stalked by large carnivorous creatures was particularly annoying for some, and many felt their sufferings, what with continual wars and genocide, outweighed the rewards of being in a physical body in a third dimensional world."

Jehran spoke. "Many of these particularly annoyed souls were very clever, but quite frankly lazy. They learned that if they refused to take on a body, and remained on the other side of physical incarnation, they could observe their fellow brother/sister souls. And while they observed, they discovered they could utilize the psychic and emotional energies emitted by those who were themselves brave enough to face 3-D experiences. Thus, the lazy ones learned to siphon off the emotions of others and use them, as energy, for their own purposes. They learned to consume emotion in order to enhance and enlarge themselves. Eventually, they learned to build kingdoms by projecting their thoughts as realities fueled by this energy; these kingdoms came to be known as heavens and hells."

Seeing that Jehran had safely introduced the part that usually stunned most humans into abject fear, Tathata again spoke up. "We enlightened beings call the kingdoms built by these groups of lazy souls the Phantasmal Hierarchies."

At this point, Thel Dar couldn't resist and interjected, "Those lazy, good-for-nothing energy-consuming loafers!"

A startled laugh of relief burst from the group.

"Wow! You mean the mind-parasites?" Michael exclaimed.

Tathata continued, "Well, in truth they are just ordinary souls like you and me who have come from other planetary systems and experiences in order to incarnate. They have merely adopted a mildly aberrant form of behavior which makes existence less pleasant for those who are caught in their deceptive *Trap*. The *Trap* resembles a thick web of frequencies, a cocoon of illusions created by thought, which can contain only those deluded by its power. You see, many of the souls who control the Phantasmal Hierarchies are not truly evil, but merely abominably indolent. In their own way, they are just as stuck in the reality of the *Trap* as those they have ensnared. Their heavens are as unreal as their hells; even the grandest heaven becomes more than a little boring after so many eons.

"Phantasmal Hierarchies can go on seemingly forever unless enlightened beings volunteer to enter a reality and break up the *Traps* these lazy tyrants have created. Entrapped civilizations occur frequently throughout all the universes, but especially in third dimensional worlds."

Jehran spoke again. "When the *Trap* is broken, the inhabitants of the Phantasmal Hierarchies have nothing left to feed on to sustain the worlds they have created. Those worlds, heavens and hells alike, collapse, and the tyrants who have ruled them are forced to incarnate somewhere.

"Many of them are now being forced to incarnate as more and more humans expand their consciousness to activate their latent DNA. This is one reason why the population of Earth is increasing dramatically."

"So the mass visions of UFOs are actually designed to help humans evolve past their isolated and limited perceptions of themselves?" Gracie asked.

"Yes," Thel Dar answered. "They also help to eliminate

121

the fear of death, because an expanded consciousness imme-diately becomes aware that Life is endless, and that death is an illusion—or rather, a transition. When humans lose their fear of death, the tyrants in the Phantasmal Hierarchies lose their most powerful weapon. If a man knows that nothing ever dies, how can he be owned or tormented?"

Inanna was beginning to understand. "My family—Anu, Enlil, and all of us, not just Marduk—were actually a part of these Phantasmal Hierarchies, weren't we?"

"Very good! I mean, truly excellent!" Thel Dar con-gratulated Inanna. "That is not an easy thing to realize about oneself or one's own family."

Inanna sighed deeply. "I guess if I had gone on winning wars and conquering territories, and following every little compulsive, selfish whim that entered my pretty little head, I never would have stopped to ask myself the *why* question."

"That is the general rule, beloved woman," Jehran said, consoling her. "You see, as painful as it was, losing Sargon, Akkad, and all of your kingdoms was the best thing that could have happened to you. I know that time was agoniz-ing for you, but see how you have evolved; you no longer need to dominate everything and everyone."

Thel Dar smiled sympathetically at Inanna. "Remember, I have *always* loved you, Inanna."

Jehran reached out to touch Inanna's delicate blue fingers. He was very proud of her for having the courage to realize that she and her family had been a part of the Phantasmal Hierarchies controlling the Earth.

Inanna was still taking in the whole ugly truth. "If Marduk hadn't defeated Anu and Enlil, they would still be using the human species as a sub-race of slaves, wouldn't they?"

"I'm afraid so," Jehran said gently. "It seems that all

souls learn only through experience. That is the beauty and the mystery of Prime Creator. That is why Life *is;* so that we may all experience."

Clarissa asked thoughtfully, "Why are there so many frightening tales about giant lizards in our mythology, all those stories of reptilian tyrants?"

"In the human body," Thel Dar answered, "which is used by most souls who incarnate into Earth's third dimensional plane, there is in the brain area a receptive gland called the reptilian brain. All those incarnating in this vehicle have a reptilian brain, and therein are lodged the receptors for survival: fight or flight. If one takes the energies of fight or flight to their logical extreme, you find tyrants and victims. Everyone in a humanoid body harbors a little latent reptilian tyrant within. The story is very familiar, on a conscious or a subconscious level, to all who have incarnated in human bodies. More evolved souls have learned to control the tyrant/victim impulses within themselves. Your cousin Marduk still has a little something to learn."

"You can say that again!" Inanna laughed, and everyone relaxed and laughed with her. They were beginning to feel at ease with their new knowledge.

Thel Dar and Tathata were pleased, knowing that a light heart opens the door to learning and wisdom. And what would be the fun of life, unless one could occasionally see humor in the small ironies woven into creation, as Prime Creator eternally danced across time and space with Its veiled Self.

Thel Dar and Tathata knew that Earth's inhabitants had a lot to learn in a short period. It was time for them to activate the *Living Waters* within their endocrine systems and to open the unused portions of their brains. Access to the diverse dimensional realities of all-the-possible worlds was the God-given right of everyone with the courage for it.

The time had come for the humans to become truly sovereign, to trust the Spirit within them, and to master discernment. This was what the New Age was all about. You can't put new wine in the old bottles; the human body itself had to be altered.

Prime Creator was ready to move on into a fresh form of expression. As the most powerful of all magicians, Prime Creator desired to expand the Divine Illusion. The beings living in third dimensional Earth were poised to push the envelope of their reality beyond the known.

For those who dared, who had the courage to move away from the old illusions, the time had come to activate their latent DNA, open the rest of the brain, and become the long-awaited enhanced data-collecting vehicles. The power of God's eternal, undying love would allow them to evolve as sovereign beings, and to begin to have a lot more fun!

The end of Part I

INTERIM:
THE LIVING WATERS

Heat wells up within me,
Searching for a place to rest,
before expanding on.
Resting to renew itself.
Hot waves of Fire undulate,
Circling through my Being.
At ONE with my Source,
I come from the FIRE that renews me.
Burning.
Blue flames kiss.
Cells ignite.
White heat expands me.
I am that I am.
I am the dream and the dreamer.
No distractions, no false note can steal me
from the Lover that consumes me.
Heat melts me, bringing me to Life.
Ah! Sweet mouth deep Within!
Open wide your lips of honey.
Let the streams of liquid Fire flow out...
The fertile Darkness waits.

I

INNER EARTH

Anu, the great-grandfather of Inanna, the patriarch of the great dynasty of Anu, realized his family had brought great suffering and devastation to the planet Earth.

After the explosion of the great radiation weapon, the Gandiva, Anu and his son Enlil were deposed as rulers of Earth and their home, Nibiru, by the tyrant Marduk and his vast armies of clones. Marduk, Anu's own grandson, hated his grandfather and his uncle Enlil. Marduk's sole desire was to rule the world. He hated his own father, Enki, perceiving poor Enki as a weakling, and felt nothing but contempt for Anu and Enlil.

Anu had retreated with Enlil to a neighboring star system to watch helplessly as Marduk poisoned the hearts and minds of the human race with relentless and insidious propaganda. It was a sad and lonely time for Anu. He had once been the proud father of a great family, and it broke his heart to watch his son Enlil's golden hair turn gray, like his own. Once a veritable god in a great dynasty, Anu now lived in exile and defeat.

Anu and Enlil wanted to regain their Nibiruan home, and to release Earth from Marduk's tyrants. Others in the Galaxy whom Marduk had displaced met with Anu and Enlil from time to time to discuss a military solution. They hoped to defeat Marduk's imposing armies.

From space, Anu had discreetly observed Inanna and the others who had dared to insert a portion of their consciousness throughout time as multidimensional selves, into the ongoing 3-D chaos of planet Earth.

Anu was made wiser from the experience of defeat. He devised a strategy to help the human race and to balance the inequities Marduk's tyrants had perpetuated throughout Earth's history. Inspired by Inanna and the others, Anu inserted himself back into time to establish his plan in Earth's third dimensional reality.

Secretly transporting himself to Inner Earth, Anu called upon his daughter, Ninhursag, who lived in the Kingdom of the Snake People. Long ago, Ninhursag and her brother Enki had created the human race. In a laboratory, they kept busy monitoring the mutant genome of the race of humans they had given birth to.

The Snake People and the Dragon People, who live in Inner Earth, had offered to protect Enki and Ninhursag. Enki's mother, Id, was a Dragon Princess. Anu had taken Id as a concubine when Earth had been colonized, to sanction a treaty between their races. The alliance allowed Anu's family to live on the surface of the Earth provided they left Id's people in peace. The match between Anu and Id had produced Enki, who had produced Marduk.

Ninhursag, with her brother Enki at her side, had devoted herself to an extensive genetic research project to test the long-term effects of radiation on the DNA of the humans living on the surface of the Earth.

When Ninhursag saw Anu, she exclaimed, "Father! You have come! How happy I am to see you."

Enki turned to look at his father, Anu; both men were aged beyond their years. Tears welled up in the eyes of Enki and ran down his aquiline nose. Embarrassed, he brushed the tears away.

"Father, what have I done? My own son, the traitor Marduk, has robbed us of everything. Can you ever forgive me?"

In spite of their differences, Anu had always loved Enki, and he now put his arms around his estranged offspring.

"My son, we must leave the past behind us. It does no good to blame each other anymore; we have both been foolish in our own way. Now is the time to think only of the race we created in bondage, and what we can do to free the humans from their invisible prison. From now on, we must work in an alliance.

"Ninhursag, my brilliant daughter," Anu inquired, "tell me that you have specimens of the original DNA from your early experiments. We need something very pure, from those first days when we placed the seeds of *Homo erectus* into our female astronauts, before we altered his blood. We need the DNA which contains the telepathic abilities of *Homo erectus*, which was not mutated by exposure to the radiation of the Gandiva."

"Why, yes, my father. You know how meticulous my scientific practices are; I save everything. I saved the original DNA from *Homo erectus* with his telepathic faculties intact, along with some of the early experimental genomes carrying those Pleiadian racial qualities impractical for a slave race. I can get them for you, if they will be useful."

"Ah, I knew you would not fail me, my daughter," Anu said. Turning to Enki, he continued, " My son, I want to see your mother, the Princess Id. I have a plan, and I need her to teach me the peaceful ways of her people. I plan to hatch a new race of beings, a race that will be impervious to the brainwashing techniques of our Marduk."

Id, Princess of the Dragon People and mother to Enki, sat alone in her dressing room. The years had left her with a soft beauty, her passions cooled, yet not extinguished. The Dragon and Snake People had lived together in peace for many years now. They were too highly evolved to engage in the adolescent acts of tyranny and war. The inhabitants of Inner Earth were far more evolved than those Nibiruans who had lived on the surface above them.

Id was recalling how, long ago, she had been given to Anu to form a covenant between the two races. Their mating had turned out well; she and Anu had shared a great passion together, and Enki had been the result.

Id had never cared for Anu's planet, Nibiru, or for the endless parties and political liaisons of his sister/wife, Antu. With Anu's consent, Id retreated into Inner Earth to be with her own people. She loved Anu and she cherished their son, Enki. But Id also recognized the hubris innate within Anu's family, and instinctively she knew where this flaw of insolent and excessive pride would lead.

In her wisdom, Id was bored by the endless power struggles of Anu's children and grandchildren. The races of Inner Earth had evolved past the frequencies of tyranny. They were telepathic, able to communicate over great distances without speaking. Both the Dragon and the Snake People knew that their apparent racial differences did not separate them. In consciousness, underneath the diversity of shapes and skin colors, they were all one, from the same source, Prime Creator.

Id had been informed that Anu was coming to see her, and she was waiting patiently for him. The two had not seen each other in what seemed like an eternity. Id wanted to look beautiful for the man who had once been greatly excited by her sexual powers. She had chosen a transparent golden gown that accented her still-smooth greenish-gold skin. The garment was cut low enough to reveal her sumptuous, firm breasts. Blood-red rubies, covering her throat, arms, and fingers, entirely harmonized with her fiery red eyes.

When Anu arrived, the sight of his princess lover brought back torrid memories. Their passion had been more than memorable. In fact, Anu had often wished for Id's company on long nights during a few of Antu's interminable diplomatic parties. Not that Anu didn't love Antu; but there was something rare and unique about Id, and their lovemaking, that Anu could never quite put aside. Perhaps those memories had contributed to his coming to her in this moment to ask for help. Id's guidance was exactly what Anu now wanted.

"Princess Id, my dearest, you are more beautiful than

ever." Anu took her jeweled hands in his, not daring to be more forward after so many years had passed between them. Her skin glowed in the candle light.

"Anu, you flatter an old woman," she replied tenderly.

"No, Id, it is I who have grown old and weary with the passing of time. Things have gone very badly for me and my family, as you well know. Perhaps, as you predicted."

"Yes, I have watched the unraveling of your family and the great rivalries between Enki, our son, and Enlil, the son born of you and your sister, Antu. What is to become of your boys, Anu, and of the human race that Enki and Ninhursag created?"

"That is why I have come to you, my princess," Anu answered. "I am here to ask for your help in creating a new race up on the Earth. From the original batch of experimental DNA, Ninhursag can begin to breed a new species which will have its natural telepathic abilities intact. I want this race to have access to the Spirit within them, and to feel, as your people do, a reverent connection with the planet they inhabit.

"I need you to guide and educate them to honor life and to communicate with the Earth itself, in the way you were educated as a young girl. We must nurture a consciousness that will be impervious to the insidiously divisive propaganda of my grandson and nemesis, the tyrant Marduk."

"But Anu, it is *you* who are the tyrant." Id spoke bluntly; Marduk was her grandson as well. Like an arrow, Id's words flew straight to Anu's heart; he knew she spoke the truth.

With great humility, he said, "Teach me to become greater than a tyrant. For the sake of my family and the human species, help me to evolve. In the memory of the love we once shared, help me, my princess."

Id smiled sweetly; she still loved him. "How can I refuse the father of my son? How can I refuse such a handsome and gentle old man?"

II

CREATING

Ninhursag immediately went to work on the DNA she had stored from so many years past. In the beginning of the genetic experiments she and Enki had performed, there was a particularly frustrating period when the embryos created in the female astronauts were entirely too intelligent and independent to suit the current needs of the family of Anu. After all, the race they were striving for had to be obedient and docile. These offspring had to be disposed of, much to the growing despair of their astronaut mothers.

The women were told regularly that they were serving their species well, and that what they did was for the good of the home planet. But being women, the astronaut mothers naturally became attached to the babies they carried within their bodies. They were not always told what happened to the unwanted experiments; nevertheless, it became harder and harder for the mothers to give their little ones up to an unknown fate. Many began to suspect what was happening when they gave birth to babies who soon disappeared, and they suffered deep emotional trauma as a consequence.

To ease her conscience, Ninhursag had managed to save the DNA from each and every child, and it was from this store that she and Enki, at Anu's request, began to create a new race of beings. The members of this race would combine the telepathic abilities of *Homo erectus* with the unaltered DNA of their creators. Ninhursag named them the Children of Anu.

The children grew up with Id presiding as their mother. Both the Dragon and the Snake People of Inner Earth sent counselors to instruct the new race in ethics, astrology, healing, basic survival skills, and rudimentary agriculture. Anu wanted them to remain in a state of pure simplicity; he realized that a culture with an advanced technology would draw the unwanted attention of Marduk's tyrants. Anu wanted his children to remain unnoticed, to leave no footprints.

Id called in the Old Serpent Woman to transmit her cosmology to the young ones. This old woman, half snake and half human, was considered the wisest being in Inner Earth. It was said that she knew everything, all of history, even that before the creation of all-the-possible worlds, beyond time. The Old Serpent Woman had once helped Inanna at a very crucial time in her life.

The Children of Anu were taught to honor Spirit within them, and thus all of life—their fellow humans, the animals upon the land, and nature herself. The trees, mountains, and rivers were to be regarded as equals, and respected as such. The origin of every act could be grounded in one thought: Everything *is* Spirit!

The Old Woman's serpent head was at first frightening to the children, but as time passed they came to love her. Images of serpents became deeply encoded into their souls' memories, and this fledgling race carried a love and respect for both the Dragons of Id and the Snake People.

At last, they were mature and ready to be transplanted into a remote area on the surface of the Earth, an ellipse of land bounded by tall mountains to the east and a great river to the west and north. There, it was hoped, they could live peacefully, to reproduce and generate an entire culture impervious to the entrapping influences of Marduk's tyranny.

The most significant ancient wisdom Anu asked Id to teach his children was the knowledge of *being-at-one* with the planet Earth, and therefore with nature herself. Anu knew that Mother Earth possessed a higher frequency than any tyrant, and that if the children faithfully attuned themselves to the vibrational frequency of this blue-and-green planet, they would be invisible to Marduk's treachery.

Id taught them that the Earth was their mother, and the sky their father. She trained them to listen intelligently to the sound of the winds and the waters. They learned to converse with the animals, the trees, and the rocks. They blessed the seeds they planted in the ground, and sought permission from the streams to take their water. Spirit and the invisible worlds were inseparably interwoven into their daily lives. For the Children of Anu, Spirit and matter were known to be one.

At last the time came; the children had grown into men and women who were now having children of their own. It was time for Anu to take them from Id's care to the surface of the planet, to the Land of the Ellipse. It was time for Anu and Id to say farewell.

Id waited alone in the dark silence of her quarters. Tomorrow, Anu would come for the children to take them to a remote area on the surface of the Earth. She would miss them; she would miss Anu. Id's lovely body filled with passion as she remembered their early days together.

Anu knocked at her door and entered. The two lovers stood face to face. They both knew that this might be the last time they would see each other. Both had been too busy to spend much time together. Anu had returned to his son Enlil while Ninhursag, Enki, and Id prepared the children.

Id had ordered a special meal prepared for their last meeting together.

Anu's heart likewise filled with memories of his old flame. As he entered her rooms, he thought, *How beautiful she looks!* The room was again softly lit with candles; and if there were any lines of age on Id's once-youthful face, Anu did not notice them. The two sat across a table laden with delicious foods fit for a Dragon princess.

"Anu, I must tell you that in my heart I have never forgotten how you made me feel when we first met. I shall miss you, old man. To me, you are the same man I fell passionately in love with so long ago. I shall think of you tenderly for all time." Tears formed in Id's fiery red eyes.

"I have been thinking the same thing, dearest Id," Anu replied softly.

Not even noticing the food spread so elegantly before them, the two lovers of old began to gaze into each other's eyes. An energy began to accumulate in the air between them. Anu thought, *There is something so inexplicably exciting about this woman. She has touched me in a way that no other can.*

Id's eyes began to burn with the heat of passion rising within her. As a member of the Dragon race, Id's ideas of lovemaking were a little different from some Pleiadian traditions, but Anu had never let that bother him.

Responding to the energies building between them, Anu and Id rose from the table and moved closer together. A strange cry came from Id's throat, a cry Anu remembered well from the old times. Id was proceeding into her "heat," and her demeanor transformed itself accordingly.

Long dragon claws began to protrude from the tips of her fingers, and her body began to pulsate with the passion that overwhelmed her. Id reached out, grabbed Anu by his shoulders, and threw him to the floor. Anu, tall and still powerful, didn't mind at all that Id easily overwhelmed him. On the contrary, the torrent of passion flowing between them rejuvenated Anu physically, mentally, and spiritually.

Anu felt incredibly alive, young again; his manhood stood erect as evidence of his feelings for his Dragon princess. Entering her, Anu gasped, "Id, my darling! It is even more wonderful than I remembered!"

Id was not listening. Dragon sounds arose in her throat as her breathing rate increased. She held Anu down with her talons as waves of ecstasy flowed over these two, melting them into one consciousness, one being. For the rest of that night, Id and Anu lost themselves in each other, floating in the forever Void with no boundaries, no bodies, and no time.

When morning came, they said farewell.

III

THE VISION
OF THE HEART

At Anu's request, Id had instructed the Snake People to construct a tunnel through which the children could travel up to the Earth's surface. The underground passage to the Land of the Ellipse was designed in such a way that it would vanish, never to reappear, once Anu had the children safely above.

Anu would not stay long with them; his frequency was too easily detected by Marduk's energy-monitoring systems. Even though Anu had generated a cloaking system for the area, he didn't want to take any unnecessary risks.

As the members of the small party emerged from the tunnel, they looked around them. The ellipse of land Anu had chosen glowed with Earth's pristine beauty. The children listened to the singing waters of a stream; the stream spread out into a small green valley bordered by tall cliffs of purple, red, and sienna sandstone. Immense clear blue skies, punctuated by an occasional gathering of billowy white clouds, blanketed the Land of the Ellipse. The place was magical in its purity, just as Anu had known it would be.

Before leaving, Anu helped the children build their first dwelling. He wanted them to have an underground refuge from potential radiation. Together, they dug deep into the earth to create a great circle sixty-four feet in diameter. Anu used the laser beam from his weapon to skillfully carve out large stones for them to arrange as walls around the circular shelter. After Anu was gone, they would have only obsidian to cut stones with; but on this day, it was necessary to hurry.

In the center of the circular dwelling, which Anu named *kiva*, he hollowed out an opening in the floor called a *sipapu*—a symbolic entryway into the world below, to remind the children of the day they had come to this place from deep within Inner Earth.

The DNA that was chosen for the children retained both the telepathic abilities of *Homo erectus* and the Pleiadian faculty which allowed access other dimensional realms. Id had taught them how to call her consciousness into their world, should they need guidance. They were also free to call upon the Old Serpent Woman, and of course, Anu.

Being telepathic, they could speak to each other *mind-to-mind* without making any sound, even across great distances; they had no need for a written language. However, Anu gave them certain sacred symbols to transmit memory from one generation to the next—to serve as a sacred bond to see them through whatever time might bring.

Anu carved these symbols into that first great kiva. One symbol, consisting of three circles set one within the other, was to remind the tribe that all-the-possible worlds lie nested within each other like the layers of an onion.

The second symbol could be seen as either lightning, a snake, or a slender spiral seen from its side. This symbol stood for the undulating cycles in creation, and for the primal force of life as it descends into the body's invisible centers, like lightning from a powerful dark storm. It also represented the helixes of the children's genetic codes, which could be charged by and infused with such energy.

The third symbol, a circle enclosing a pictogram of a flying eagle, was an abstraction of Anu's old symbol for Nibiru, the planet he had lost to his nemesis, Marduk. The symbol meant *home* to these children, because half of their genome had been extracted from the inhabitants of Nibiru.

Nibiru's symbol, the basis for the eagle pictogram, displayed four propellers emitting scaler energy. Originally this had been the technical symbol for scaler energy; Nibiru itself emitted great amounts of radiation which could be converted into scaler waves. The abstraction of an eagle would serve the Children of Anu well, helping them to remember their origins. The circle would remind them that at the close of this cycle, Anu would return.

When he had finished cutting the three symbols into the stone walls of the kiva, Anu turned to the children he cherished, who were now grown. There were twelve adult males, twelve adult females, and a few little children. Some of the females were pregnant. Anu looked tenderly at this small, vulnerable band of humans.

"My beloved children," Anu said, "the time has come for me to say farewell to you. Remember always to use the Vision of the Heart. Such vision will guard you and serve you well as you and your descendants move out into this sacred land. The Vision of the Heart will keep you safe from any enemy. As long as you are able to see with your heart, your frequencies will resonate beyond those who would harm you.

"This will be an extraordinary adventure for you all. Your numbers will grow. Many courageous souls will desire to incarnate in the bodies of your precious children, in order to experience their remarkable genetic code, and to enjoy the challenges of living in this magical place. You are endowed with the wisdom of the Old Serpent Woman, the nurturing love of Id, and the great purity of the Spirit within you. Earth herself will embrace you with her abundance as you honor her.

"I only wish it were possible for me to remain here with you. Alas, I have other tasks to complete, and my genome would be a beacon inviting trouble to this unnoticed ellipse of purple and red stones. But my spirit will be with you in the winds."

At that moment, Anu became aware of a young woman in the early stages of pregnancy. She was handsome and strong, with velvet-smooth brown skin. Anu respectfully gazed into her eyes, and for a perfect moment basked in the light of her soul. He thought, *Ah, how sweet it would be to take abode in that womb, to become her child.*

And so Anu decided that like Inanna and the others, he would soon project a portion of himself into this graceful woman. One day he would call her mother. He smiled fondly at her as he began to descend the spiraling tunnel that would lead him back into Inner Earth, to the Time Portal protected by the Dragon People—to await transport to the neighboring star system.

The entryway closed behind Anu, leaving his children alone in a strange new land.

IV

EXILE

The orbiting space station that had once encircled the planet Earth, serving as an intermediary location between Nibiru and Earth, was now poised in the infinite darkness of space—waiting. The station itself was of titanic proportions: Layer upon layer of living, working modules extruded themselves into the blackness. Pleiadian technology made use of "living" cellular metals that did not wear or erode with time; the flawless perfection of the orbiting space station had not been marred by its exile.

Standing on the primary receiving deck, Enlil impatiently awaited the return of his father, Anu. The station had been their only home since Marduk had taken Earth for himself. Enlil had never approved of certain tendencies in the human species, but Earth had been his domain, and he was determined to deliver her inhabitants from the hands of the reptilian tyrants in general, and Marduk in particular.

Enlil had repeatedly forewarned his half-brother Enki about Marduk. It had been obvious to Enlil through the years that Enki was losing control over his firstborn son. Marduk had developed an insidious form of mind control over his followers and his father. Enki stubbornly refused to listen to Enlil; Enlil's warning had been only grist for the mill in the brothers' ceaseless sibling rivalry.

Anu's ship safely landed in the station's port; as Anu stepped out onto the deck, Enlil embraced his father.

"Father, I am relieved to see you."

"My son, how are you?" Anu inquired, looking closely at Enlil. The fact that Enlil's shining golden hair was turning gray, like his own, always had an unsettling effect on Anu. Was it a sign that time was marching on, even for Pleiadians?

Enlil said, "I am well, and Mother is anxious to see you. How goes your mission?"

"Excellently!" Anu replied. "My son, I have decided to join Inanna and the others in the adventure of incarnating into the human body! I will project a portion of myself into the womb of a woman in my beloved tribe."

Enlil had his doubts about the human race; he frankly wasn't sure the species had a viable future at all.

"Father, are you certain you know what you are doing? Look what has happened to the courageous Inanna in her various incarnations. You will be so vulnerable. Are you certain you want to go through that? Being lost in a human body can be treacherous."

Anu answered eagerly, "If you had but stood there with me in that magical place, the steep cliffs rising above us to a perfect blue sky, and felt the warm sun, the gentle breeze…as I listened to the singing rivers, I looked deeply into the shining clear eyes of this new race Ninhursag and Enki created in their laboratories. Id has given them great wisdom. The purity of their hearts and minds is like a magnet to me, and I long to join them, to enter into Life with them and experience whatever comes."

Enlil thought to himself, *Oh no, not Id again.* "Better you than me, Father. I have yet to see a human body I would wish even a part of myself to inhabit."

Enlil had always been a perfectionist, rigid and a little judgmental in his innate righteousness. But in a family comprised of chaotically self-centered adventurers, Enlil's adherence to principle and to the fulfillment of duty was a welcome balancing force.

"Perhaps one day you will change your mind, my son. One day, you may join us upon the Earth in a very human body, just for the fun of such a new experience."

Anu smiled at Enlil. He had always been proud of his favorite son and he loved him greatly; Enlil was really so much like his mother, Antu.

"Come, now we will go to see your mother."

Antu's rooms were like her—rich with elegance and power. The years had been kind to this impressive matriarch. Her beauty was heightened by an unwavering confidence. Completely sure of herself in every moment, Antu possessed a majestic grace rarely seen in the women of Earth. She was truly a queen; her royal dignity emanated from within and was not dependent on her circumstances.

Antu viewed this recent shift in her status—being

obliged to "camp out," as it were, on the orbiting space station—as merely a temporary setback. She could not accept the idea that little Marduk, Enki's ill-behaved first-born son, could possibly be a permanent threat to the life she had known.

Even as a child Marduk had been especially unruly, given to tormenting the other children with his terrible games. Antu, like her precious Inanna, had never liked Marduk. A sense of duty had once impelled her to show him the occasional outward display of affection, lest people gossip, thinking Antu was jealous of Marduk's grandmother, Id. Quite the contrary: Antu had never been jealous of Anu's concubines. She found such a trivial emotion as jealousy to be ridiculous; she did not require it. Antu felt completely confident that Anu needed her to assist him with the strategic decisions and intergalactic liaisons so necessary to their lives—she was sure she was irreplaceable. And indeed Anu would not have been himself without Antu. He keenly appreciated her diplomatic skills, and knew that the superficial glitter of all those elaborate parties masked the work of a brilliant politician.

The moment Anu walked in to greet her, Antu knew that things had gone exactly as she had foreseen; he had been with Id, and they had made love. Antu smiled, embracing her husband/brother.

"Anu, welcome home."

"My dearest wife," Anu said warmly. "How I have missed you and your great counsel."

In her heart, Antu knew no woman could ever take him away from her; and, more to the point, why would she want to control Anu's life anyway? Manipulated, predictable behavior would bore her. Was not Prime Creator, through

Anu, expressing and experiencing life in all its fullness? Antu saw her life as abundant in family, friends, and love; Anu's return was evidence of that, and she had not doubted him.

Anu sank down among a profusion of silken pillows to enjoy a snifter of Arcturian brandy, while Antu placed delicious comestibles before him.

"My darling, you must be tired and hungry," she said.

"Antu, I am so anxious to tell you all that has happened. The children have progressed wonderfully, and I have a plan I am sure you will applaud."

It was almost midnight in the Land of the Ellipse. The moonless sky was so thick with stars as to make the Earth itself luminous. A pregnant young woman was at the end of her labor; as the child forced himself from her body, the woman stared up at the stars above her. A voice cried out in the night—the voice of a newborn baby boy.

The midwife cleaned the child and handed him to his weary, happy mother. In her thoughts, the mother spoke to those around her. *We shall call him Filled-with-Stars in honor of this night.* Her husband nodded in agreement.

A song rang out from the tribe of the Children of Anu, and it echoed up and off the cliffs surrounding them. The song was one of joy and gratitude; a baby had been born. Another soul had entered their world to be cherished by them, to share their lives, and to love them in return.

His mother placed her full breast into Filled-with-Stars' hungry mouth, and as she suckled him, the silent stars above looked on.

V

PARTIES

Around the turn of the last millennium, Marduk and his followers were very busy. There was a lot to do— so many wars to foment, so many religions to corrupt. Marduk saw that the ascent of tyrants and their empires was progressing splendidly. There was virtually no occurrence that he and his reptilian tyrants could not somehow turn to their advantage. It was a game of sorts; the human species was almost too easy to manipulate, succumbing with little provocation to a profound state of confusion.

All over the planet, humans blindly followed one belief system or charismatic leader after another; then abruptly, frequently, like schools of fish, they turned to chase yet another creed or despot. Minority populations became scapegoats; a difference in skin color, religion, or language could rouse the majority to commit the most terrifying atrocities.

The fear of death drove many humans to a peculiar obsession, to the overwhelming compulsion to force everyone to believe identical dogmas. This gave them a false sense of confidence. People wanted to know that everyone was inevitably going to the very same hell, or heaven; they felt more comfortable in a shared hopelessness. Religious persecution was rampant and reached new heights during the Inquisition.

Immutable adherence to belief systems based on fear was providential for Marduk—it seemed to motivate humans to inflict nearly unimaginable acts of torture and torment upon their fellow creatures. They were so resourceful at dreaming up methods of inflicting excruciating pain on one another that Marduk didn't even have to spend his valuable time encouraging them. He found the grisly business of religious persecution to be an extremely efficient producer of the kind of psychic food he and his cloned legions thrived on.

Marduk rather enjoyed spending time on Nibiru. He had, with some relish, taken over Antu's grand pavilions, and he had redecorated the palace, in what might be called the evil-empire style, to suit his own tastes. Numerous entryways, all of which led to over-sized statues of himself, were lined with severe black and gold ornament. References to his genius, to his strategic brilliance, to his handsome countenance, and even, god help us, to his poetry, were everywhere. In Antu's once tastefully adorned ballrooms, Marduk presided like the Mad Hatter over endless parties. They weren't the sort Antu would ever have wanted to attend; all of his parties were in honor of Marduk.

So busy was Marduk that he wasn't paying much

attention to an obscure area in the western hemisphere of the planet Earth. There had been no reason for him to notice a small group of somewhat primitive souls living on an ellipse of land in the southwestern section of the North American continent. There was no evidence of a civilization there important enough to attract his observations; and so the Children of Anu, with a little cloaking assistance from Inner Earth, went unnoticed in their new home for quite a long and peaceful period of time.

In the Land of the Ellipse, the tribe of the Children of Anu flourished and grew. The boy-child named Filled-with-Stars was dearly loved by his family and the members of his tribe. Even as a young boy, Filled-with-Stars was by tribal assent recognized as a natural leader; the first to be born after arriving from Inner Earth, he was said to "walk with" an innately powerful wisdom.

Filled-with-Stars had been the first to suggest that the tribe hollow out the caves in the high cliffs above. He had observed that the stone cliffs which faced the afternoon sun absorbed heat from the low-arching winter sunlight; the caves would be warm. A wise, handsome old man came to Filled-with-Stars as a guardian and told him that the caves would also protect the tribe from the evil effects of the radiation which rained from the sky from time to time.

The tribe had brought with them dried foods to eat and seeds to plant, enough for seven years. The families of Inner Earth had supplied them well for their undertaking.

The little group was lonely without their mother, Id; they all looked forward to their gatherings in the kiva.

There Id and the Old Serpent Woman rose up out of the sipapu as transparent beings. The Children of Anu celebrated and sang while Id comforted them with loving memories, and the Old Serpent Woman imparted her much-needed wisdom.

Though Id was of the Dragon race and the Old Serpent Woman from the Snake People, they both thoroughly enjoyed their excursions to the surface together. Projecting their spirit bodies into the kiva was a great adventure for them. Both loved to be present at births, and when Id first saw Filled-with-Stars, she laughed with delight, immediately recognizing her lover Anu. *What a daring soul*, she thought to herself, wondering if, or when, she would join him.

On starry nights, with a fire flickering soft light on the stone walls of the kiva, the Old Serpent Woman taught the children and their children: *Everything is Spirit.* She taught them about the forever Void, about how beingness comes from non-beingness.

"This Earth, the Universe, and all-the-possible worlds are formed of Spirit, and must be honored as such. Everything in nature is vibrant with life. Learn to speak with the birds and the gentle deer. Whisper to the steep cliffs and the stones that sing. Wrap your arms around the majestic trees as the winds caress them, and listen carefully to the laughing waters that run through your canyon.

"Polarities in all things allow the appearance of separation; everything contains its opposite. But in truth, *all is one.* Light and shadow, male and female, good and evil, positive and negative—all function to allow the holographic matrix of your world. In time, through observation, the cyclical dance of apparent polarities grows predictable. As your wisdom increases in such *knowingness*, you may long to transcend the illusion of appearances; but for now, enjoy them and learn from them.

"There is no need to control or interfere with the perceptions of another; Prime Creator experiences in us all, expressing Its infinite forms. The one who chooses to simply allow the cycles is wise indeed. Let everyone play; we meet, inevitably, in the same place."

After the Old Serpent Woman had spoken, everyone enjoyed delicious honeycakes and the juice of berries that grew abundantly on the hillsides. Being in the kiva together at night, watching the firelight dance on the curved walls, and later, walking home together under the stars, their tummies filled with cakes—these shared experiences created feelings that invisibly wove the tribe together.

Time passed and Filled-with-Stars grew to be a man. He was skilled at the hollowing out of the caves high in the cliffs, which were expanded to keep the tribe warm in winter. He and many others had grown accustomed to scampering up and down the sheer cliff faces like little monkeys. No one ever fell; in fact, for fun, the tribe held races. No one was ever declared the sole winner in these games. Loving each other, the tribe members honored all the runners, recognizing each for his or her degree of skill—and running up the sides of the great cliff was fun!

One night, Filled-with-Stars took a walk up to the mountain spring over and beyond the cliffs. The moon was full, and he wanted to see its reflection in the small pool formed by the spring.

Arriving at the moonlit pool, Filled-with-Stars saw

that someone else was already there. A young woman knelt over the waters with a basket in her hands. She dipped the tightly woven basket into the pool and poured water out on the cool grass. She was surrounded by three deer, a doe and two fawns. Filled-with-Stars' arrival startled them.

"Who is there?" the young girl called out.

Moving closer to her, Filled-with-Stars was overwhelmed. The girl was so lovely; the moonlight that graced her hair seemed to shine right out of her eyes. He then recognized her as one of the earth-born children he had grown up with; but he had never seen her like this. Had the luminescence of the moon magically transformed her somehow? Her small perfect breasts made shadows on her tunic, and her hands were fine and strong.

"It is I—Filled-with-Stars. I did not mean to interrupt you. Why do you pour water on the grass?"

"I catch the moon in my basket, and pour it out for the deer to drink."

Filled-with-Stars furrowed his brows and looked closely. It was true; as she lowered the basket into the pool, the moon seemed to be captured within it. And as she poured the water out, for a moment the moon's reflection was magically suspended in the flowing water before it sank into the grass.

"I will call you Moonwaters," he said tenderly. "Let me walk you home."

The two headed toward the tribe, taking as long as they possibly could. And on that moonlit night, they shared their dreams.

Filled-with-Stars told her of the dreams in which a wise and handsome old man came to him. He said the old man lived in the stars and flew in great ships across the Universe.

Moonwaters had no trouble believing that. The Dragon Princess, Id, often appeared to the girl in her dream state and revealed insightful wisdom to her. Moonwaters shared a few of her most cherished visions with Filled-with-Stars, but she did not tell him that Id had foretold of their meeting this night. She knew to keep this in her heart, a secret.

At the door of her home, Filled-with-Stars shyly touched her hand and said good-bye; but from now on, neither would ever be alone again.

VI

TWO DRAGONS

There was no moon at all, and the stars ignited the sky above them as Gracie, Wolfie, Clarissa, and Michael made their camp in the high desert. Gracie's dogs were howling at the coyotes.

Michael had inspired the trip by filling their heads with stories of an ancient race that was said to have flourished here and then vanished, leaving only the ruins of its dwellings and wonderful pictograms in the caves of nearby cliffs as evidence of their existence. In the folklore of the Southwest, there were many stories about this ancient race of beings who had inhabited the Land of the Ellipse, but no one really knew who they were, or why they had left so abruptly.

Michael had met a few stalwart souls who had ventured to camp out in the ruins; feeling a strong presence of the vanished tribe, they had seen strange visions. Even the archeologists who had dug there reported that they could feel the past all around them. Michael was sure that the Land of the Ellipse was some kind of interdimensional opening; here was a weakness in the evanescent line of time which separated the worlds.

Wolfie cut up some dead wood and built a fire. His new body knew all about camping. After all, its previous owner was a real backwoods man who had lived alone for months at a time in the deepest parts of the Pacific Northwest forests. Wolfie, by inclination cultured and somewhat spoiled, found he could now easily put up tents, chop firewood, and engage in all kinds of activities he had never considered in his life as a musician.

Gracie, Wolfie, and Clarissa sat around the campfire listening to Michael, who was deep into his stories about the mysterious disappearance of the tribe that had once lived in the Land of the Ellipse. The firelight danced shadows across their faces.

"Some believe these ancient ones were so pure, and so aligned with nature and the Earth, that they raised their vibrational frequency to such heights that we can no longer perceive them."

Clarissa exclaimed, "Wow! You mean they are still here, but we can't see them?"

"Something like that," Michael said. "Or perhaps there is no *here*. If thought creates reality, then time and distance are only thoughts. If we could alter our consciousness to a higher vibration, conceivably time, distance, and this place would disappear for us. The tribe might be right here, resonating frequencies now to those sensitive enough to receive them; and simultaneously they could be beyond our

Galaxy in another dimensional world. Maybe the Mind of Prime Creator is a vast blackness, a forever Void where time and space cannot exist except as thought."

Wolfie was fascinated. "Back in Vienna, I often felt I was transcending time and space, while in the midst of passionately creating my music. This incongruity often occurred to me—if music, as a sound frequency, takes place in time, where does it go once the music is released? Does it proceed to move in timelines, or does it enfold upon itself, or does it cease to exist except as ink on paper?"

Wolfie had lost them on that thought, and everyone was quiet. So Wolfie threw more wood on the fire, and Michael continued his story.

"The members of this ancient tribe *knew* life had been created for them. Life was meant to be lived in joy. They loved and honored Spirit within each other, within the children they brought into this dimensional reality. The five senses were to be enjoyed: To listen to the wind, to taste the sweet waters, to smell the good earth, to feel the warmth of the sun, to see the stars up above—these things were their birthright. The members of the tribe saw themselves as extensions of their Creator, experiencing the world as it had been given to them.

"Life was movement, and the ever-changing cycles of creation were sacred. While they lived here in the Land of the Ellipse, they drank fully of each moment, understanding that one day the Portals of Time would open and they would pass into another realm. They, like all souls, would join their ancestors in the Land of the Immortals. The *when* did not matter; what mattered was to be present to life and the potential for joy in the *now*."

Gracie said softly, "I feel as if I can see them and hear

them singing in this canyon."

"Tomorrow let's go and explore the caves," Clarissa suggested.

"Good idea. Let's take our time," Michael said. He was hoping to see a UFO, and he wanted his friend, the Commander, to show up again.

As the fire died down, the little group crawled into their sleeping bags. The two dogs lay snuggled together near Gracie. One by one, the friends drifted toward sleep under the pristine night sky. A shooting star fell across Gracie's sight just as she closed her eyes. *Ah! A good omen,* she thought to herself.

✳

As a sign of his intentions, Filled-with-Stars had slept out under the open sky near Moonwaters' family home for eleven nights. He knew that they were destined to be together, and that they would have many fine children. He aspired to show her family how much he loved her. It was a great pleasure for Filled-with-Stars to sleep out under the sky he was named for.

On this night, the stars were so bright they made the Earth luminescent. Filled-with-Stars found it hard to fall asleep; when he closed his eyes, his head was filled with light. He kept seeing his beloved Moonwaters and wishing she were lying there in his arms. Lately he desired nothing so much as merely to be close to her, to gaze into her deep dark eyes. The thought of her intoxicating scent and her long silken hair threw him into joy, and kept him from sleep.

At last, late into the night, with the stars still in his eyes, this persevering lover fell into a twilight sleep. In the

160

mist, Filled-with-Stars saw a giant of a man standing beside a sensuous woman with golden-green skin. Her red eyes blazed with passion. Filled-with-Stars recognized her as Id, the Dragon Princess and guardian of his tribe. The great man was handsome, with penetrating eyes and long gray hair. Filled-with-Stars recognized him as the same old man who came to him so often in dreams.

The couple sent pulsating waves of loving energy into Filled-with-Stars. Together, they filled him with *knowing* and strength.

Then they disappeared, and the dream changed dramatically. A great nothingness filled everything. At first there was only blackness itself; and then the infinite night was suffused with a rolling mist, and an evanescent force spun phosphorous clouds into the dreamer's consciousness.

From the heart of the clouds, two immense dragons emerged. One was golden like the sun, with long purple talons and radiant scales that rippled with muscle; the dragon's brightness was blinding, and fire spewed from his mouth with every breath. The second dragon was like moonlight; silver scales covered her body. Her eyes glowed as red as her long talons. In the silence she waited—still, alert, and without fear.

Then it began. Like a primeval storm, the Moon Dragon assailed the Sun Dragon. Their fiery passions inflamed the silent emptiness surrounding them. As they undulated in vaporous flames and rolled in crackling thunder, the two brought forth all-the-possible worlds: the layered dimensions of heavens, universes, galaxies, planets, and nature herself.

From their lovemaking the two dragons brought Life into being. The undifferentiated energies of the golden

Sun Dragon found form through the matrix of the silver Moon Dragon.

Filled-with-Stars, in his Dream of Dragons, learned that the origin of life was in the playground of Prime Creator.

The stars began to fade and Filled-with-Stars blinked at the rising sun. Moonwaters emerged from the home of her parents. She embraced her husband-to-be.

"Beloved!" she cried. "I have had a dream. The dream gave me an understanding of the creation of all life."

"A dream of two dragons?" he asked hopefully.

"How did you know?" she cried.

Wrapping his arms around her, Filled-with-Stars answered, "We will be married soon, my darling. I know."

Michael was the first to wake in the morning light. He was trying to remember a very strange dream, when Clarissa suddenly sat up and began enthusiastically describing the fantastic creatures she had just encountered.

Her excitement woke the others, and incredibly, each of the four had that night dreamed the identical dream.

"There was this really huge golden dragon with..." Clarissa began.

"With long purple talons?" Michael asked.

"Why, yes. How did you know? And then there was another dragon with silver scales and..."

"Burning red eyes," Gracie interjected.

"And they made love!" Wolfie exclaimed. "But their love was thunder and lightning, a primeval passion that rolled out rhythms of creative force."

"Yes!"

They all began to laugh at the wonder of a shared dream—a dream of cosmic proportions and enlightenment. This magical canyon truly was enchanted. Here the walls of time and space had disappeared.

VII

REAL LOVE

Deep in the infinite potential of the forever Void, Thel Dar rolled over, spraying an effulgence of photons in every direction. Inhaling to pull *beingness* up into a spiral, the radiant-light Being enfolded energy in a tight and compact focus of emptiness. Holding the focus for a no-time, Thel Dar exhaled and released whirling resplendent vapors—seeds of potential—into the surrounding vast blackness. Like raindrops falling through space, colorful geometric shapes of light sallied forth as thought forms for attuned waiting receivers.

In the immense silence, Thel Dar wondered at all-the-possible worlds. In one layer of reality, Inanna and her lover Jehran had become pure thought moving across dimensional worlds to the place of Jehran's origin. By changing focus a few degrees, Thel Dar saw, in another layer of existence, Anu incarnating among his beloved children in the Land of the Ellipse. Another precise shift of focus brought Gracie and her friends into view; they were sharing the Dream of Dragons.

In another layer, the Etherian Mother Ship formed itself in Thel Dar's sight. Within the ship, the Lady of the Garnets and the Commander observed the progress of their multidimensional selves on the planet Earth. The Etherians themselves were absorbed in monitoring the machinations of the tyrant Marduk; they marked the depth of his violation of the universal Law of Non-Interference. The Etherians, while sensing Thel Dar's focus, calmly continued their work.

Thel Dar was about to inhale once more when a small but forceful presence in the forever Void made itself known. The radiant-light Being prepared to meet the visitor. It was Olnwynn, the handsome Irish warlord. One of Inanna's multidimensional selves had managed to come to Thel Dar, alone and unassisted.

"Greetings, Olnwynn. I am pleased to see you have discovered how to reach this place on your own. You are evolving, my son, waking up from your experience of barbaric wars; and I see you are in a state of love."

Olnwynn answered, "Yes, my friend, it is the power of love that has brought me here to you. Diana, who was my wife during the time I was a king on the Earth, is now in a terrible prison. Her frail body is guarded by devils dressed in white who use drugs to confine her and render her senseless. I want to free her; I want to be her knight in shining armor, to rescue her from harm."

Thel Dar spoke. "You once harmed her yourself, is that not so?"

"Ah, yes," Olnwynn replied. "It is true, and well I rue those days. It was the drink and my own foul temper that imprisoned her then. Now I see my chance to release her and redeem myself. I love Diana."

"It is the force of your love that will free her. Return to her prison, and focus your love into a weapon of liberation. See for yourself, my friend, what miracles you can perform with an astral sword in your powerful loving hands."

Thel Dar loosened its form and, falling apart before Olnwynn's eyes, evaporated.

Olnwynn floated alone for a time in the infinite blackness, trying to remember the radiant-light Being's exact words, as if they were a charm. He had come this far, but now he wondered how to get back to the bleak hospital where his wife lay captive. Then he thought to invoke the memory of the rich, soft leather in Diana's over-sized luxury car, and immediately Olnwynn found himself flung into the back seat with his brother. Brent had been sleeping, and he woke with a jolt.

"Come, brother!" Olnwynn exclaimed. "We have work to do."

The sun was shining in the clear blue sky as Gracie, Wolfie, Clarissa, and Michael hiked up into the cliffs above their camp. There were so many caves to explore, and time had ceased to matter to them. In one of the larger caves, the friends discovered pictures of spirals and snakes on the ceilings above them; enraptured, they sat down to contemplate the pictograms.

As they sat in silence, focusing, listening to the winds blow through the canyon beneath them, subtle vapors began to form in the center of the cave. An old woman who was half serpent, half human appeared. She spoke to them as though they were the former inhabitants of the canyon, as though she already knew them and had come to them out of habit.

"There is a twilight vision of the in-between," the old woman said. "Go there, and you will see the eternal Eye that exists between this world and the Other. Through the eternal Eye you may see, as it does, all-the-possible worlds as holograms, generated by shooting photons into geometric lattices as sets of vibrational frequencies. Nothing is solid; nothing is finite. There is no beginning, nor any end.

"Outside all dimensional worlds," she continued, "the Eye pulsates as it breathes cyclical rhythms into the layered frequencies of existence. Using DNA to collect experiential data as inherited lines of memory, the Source projects itself in various body formations—purely for the adventure of expressing itself through the accumulated memory of specific DNA. You four, for example.

"But you are not your bodies. The body exists only as a hologram; it is a vehicle you inhabit, the result of accumulated memory and thought. You appear to be separate in these bodies, and unique in the expressions of your individual consciousness; but behind the eternal Eye, you all originate from the same Source. You are all linked by the power of Prime Creator's Love. Life is the playing out of all potential probabilities within the Mind of God."

✳

Olnwynn and Brent stood in the hospital ward beside Diana's bed. She was so heavily drugged on this day that her two husbands were having difficulty connecting with her awareness.

"Diana! Wake up!" Brent shouted from his etheric body.

"Hear, hear, my love," Olnwynn pleaded. "You must gather yourself from this fog. We have come for you."

"What do you mean, *your* love?" Brent was getting agitated. "Diana is *my* wife, you numskull!"

"She was my wife before she was your wife, you dimwit lout!" Olnwynn reached out to wake Diana.

"Keep your hands off of her, flea brain!" Brent was enraged with jealousy.

The two men's anger brought Diana out of her stupor.

"Will both of you keep quiet!" Diana moaned. "Oh my, what a headache."

Brent pleaded with her. "Diana, listen. You can't go on like this. Soon you won't even be conscious enough to leave your body and go shopping. You'll be stuck here, a drugged zombie, your body riddled with tubes."

"That doesn't sound very nice," she murmured. "But how can I escape? I can no longer walk, and even if I could, the nurses and guards would stop me."

Olnwynn, mustering up all of his strength, remembered what Thel Dar had told him—that the power of his love could become a great sword. He began to replay as vivid memory his passionate desire for Diana, when they had first fallen in love. The memory of his feelings for her in those days, and the heated excitement they had shared, generated an energy that allowed Olnwynn to create a sword of light. Forming in his hands, the sword glowed brightly in the ethers surrounding them.

"What is that?" Diana asked.

"It is my love for you, Diana. Now listen. You must concentrate very hard. Think of leaving your body in the same way you have learned to go shopping. Focus intently, and project yourself out of your body and into that place you are so fond of, the room with the beautiful gowns. Do it now, my dearest one," Olnwynn said. "By all your will, do it!"

Diana sighed. Why was Olnwynn bothering her so? She felt tired, foggy; too tired, she was sure, to do anything at all.

"DO IT NOW!" Olnwynn commanded, marshaling all the love he had within his heart. "Do it, my love, so you can become free, and because I love you still."

Diana thought, *That was sweet.* Well, all right, she would try. She drew upon all her remaining store of energy, and, with enormous effort, flung her etheric self up and away from the fragile, shrinking body tethered to plastic tubes— and headed straight for the evening gowns in couture.

At that moment, Olnwynn saw Diana's silver cord flash by, and he shouted to Brent, "Grab it!"

Brent held fast to Diana's lifeline, the silver cord that held her in this prison of boredom. Olnwynn, as in the days of his youth in a faraway Ireland, raised the sword of light high above him—and in one sweeping thrust, cut the line.

There was an explosion! All three hurtled through non-existent space head-over-heels and, much to their surprise, landed in a cottage garden abundant with blooming flowers and songbirds. Brent, Olnwynn, and Diana looked at each other in amused bewilderment, and then began to laugh. Diana was free!

In the hospital ward, the nurses rushed in and then called the doctors, who attempted, to no avail, to bring Diana back into the abandoned shell that once had been her body.

The following day in the Pacific Northwest, Gracie's answering machine picked up a message: Her mother had passed away peacefully.

That night in the canyon with the stars above them, Wolfie lay warm beside Gracie. As he looked into her eyes, gently caressing her face and touching her hair, he thought about his old life as Wolfgang Amadeus Mozart. In those days, he had taken delight in the game of seduction; he had enjoyed many beautiful ladies.

Gracie was somehow different; he felt that their relationship was something sacred. He didn't look at her in the same way he had regarded other women. He wanted intimacy, but not just the physical kind. He had known plenty of that! With Gracie, he wanted an intimacy of the soul.

Gracie had lived alone for a long time, and was happy that her new friend wanted to proceed slowly. Wolfie was so tender and sweet with her. She had never known anyone like him; his spontaneity and childlike curiosity were a delight to her.

Ever since her experiences on Lost Mountain, Gracie saw her relationships with men in a new light. Something had changed within her soul.

After having lived in New York City for twenty years, Gracie had moved to the mountains in the Pacific Northwest. Alone in a cabin in a small mountain valley with only her beautiful dogs for company, she listened to the silence of the great cedar forest, watched the stars in the midnight sky, and learned how much more to life there is than can be perceived by the five senses.

There on Lost Mountain, Gracie had opened herself up to an expanded understanding of the apparent world. She learned to communicate with Inanna and the radiant-light Being Thel Dar. Remembering her so-called past lives, Gracie accessed the wisdom her *selves* had to offer, and her fusion with them led to a new understanding. Looking beyond the tightly drawn veils of an imposing illusion, Gracie *knew* that she was, in the ultimate sense, one with everything and everyone who had ever been or was yet to be. *Knowing* that Oneness drew her into a boundless encounter with the Love which sustains all-the-possible worlds, and changed Gracie forever.

Realizing her true relationship to life had taught her to *allow*. She didn't need to force anything; whatever was meant to be between Wolfie and her would happen in its own time. Meanwhile, she was enjoying their innocent, childlike affection for one another.

Wolfie snuggled closer to Gracie; he put his arm around her and they fell asleep. Gracie dreamed, and in the dream, her mother, Diana, came to her and spoke.

"Gracie, I have moved on. I have left the body you have known as your mother for the last time. Do not be sad; I am with friends, and I am happy to be free of that place. Do not grieve for me.

"From this side, Gracie, I see things clearly. I love you, and I wish you to be happy, to find love, and to have children of your own, if you want to. Do not use me as an excuse to be afraid of life. Life is to be lived and learned from. Everyone makes mistakes, that is how we learn. Go and be happy. Farewell, my little girl. Remember, I will always love you."

Gracie awoke, tears streaming down her face.

"Wolfie, my mother has died," she whispered in the night.

"I know." Wolfie pulled her close.

VIII

QUANTUM LEAP

Anu and Id incarnated seven times together in the Land of the Ellipse in the bodies of the tribe they had fostered. Living in harmony with the forces of nature, and in love with each other, the two had many children and shared many adventures.

Enlil watched his father's sojourns with great interest. After a time Enlil overcame his reluctance to join in, and decided to incarnate with Anu and Id. Although the tribe had not as yet devised the wheel and no carts even existed, Enlil began to build roads. Compulsively, he laid out hundreds of miles of perfectly engineered roads. Compelled by his very nature to create infrastructure, he also directed a variety of building projects. However, after that lifetime, Anu gently suggested to his son that he might be happier if he simply observed from the satellite with his mother, Antu.

The years passed and the Land of the Ellipse endured, cloaked by an invisible energy field generated by the Dragon and Snake People. More and more souls came to incarnate in this wonderful place; they were drawn as by magnets to live in the magical body-vehicles Ninhursag and Enki had created in their laboratory. The tribe's DNA was abundant with possibilities; this rare genome was very attractive to those souls who sought a diversity of experience. The plateau's population was rapidly increasing.

Not only were there more and more people inhabiting the Land of the Ellipse, but the evolution of their vibrational frequency was not like that of ordinary humans. The tribe emitted an energy pulse that was closer to Anu's rate of vibration—an energy familiar to Marduk, and potentially detectable by him. Eventually, the cloaking device was no longer sufficient to hide the magical kingdom of the Land of the Ellipse.

In the 1300s Earth time, Marduk had arranged an entertainment for himself. He set into motion a little ice age—nothing big enough to cover the entire planet, but enough to disrupt agriculture and create severe food shortages. The ensuing waves of famine caused the humans' immune systems to break down, making way for bubonic plague, or the Black Death, as it came to be known. Marduk was delighted by this amusing development.

The Black Death reduced the population of Europe by a third. Economic and military ravages accompanied the devastation, leaving survivors fearful and especially prey to superstition. On the European continent, the country known as España began to rise up and develop into a great power.

España, or Spain, sent its merciless conquerors to the New World. Callous men like Cortés and Pizarro brought religion and the sword to the Indians living across the great ocean in the western hemisphere—along with tyranny, disease, and death.

Anu foresaw that the time would come when these heartless conquerors would find their way to his tribe. The weather patterns in the Land of the Ellipse were beginning to change, and an unusual series of droughts was causing general concern. It occurred to Anu that Marduk, not wanting to interfere in a more direct and obvious manner, might have arranged to tamper with the weather patterns over this area.

Marduk had, in fact, recently been informed by his minions that an oddly familiar frequency was being tracked in a desert in the southwestern sector of the North American continent. The report suggested that a cloaking device blanketed the area, protecting it from a more thorough investigation.

Marduk sensed that something was amiss; he could always smell a rat, and his contemptible, rotten relatives were doubtless up to no good again.

With Earth securely clutched in the iron claws of fear, Marduk transported his entourage to a remote planet in the Pleiades for a holiday of sorts. The plague had devastated the Old World, and the Spanish conquistadors were successfully sacking, butchering, and pillaging the ancient Indian cultures of the New World. Marduk's master plan was running smoothly, and there wasn't much to occupy his attention. So he had flown to a lovely planet for a little vacation.

Before Marduk conquered most of the Pleiades, this small celestial body had been a relaxing resort for lovers and families to enjoy. The place was famous for its turquoise beaches and warm lavender-blue waters. Lavish gardens of exotic flowers had been brought in from all across the galaxies to enhance the pleasures of weary travelers.

With the exception of his entourage, which in reality was nothing more than a few servants, Marduk had expelled everyone from the planet. He greedily wanted it all for himself, and he appropriated an entire resort for his accommodations. One particular hotel had been the favorite of many Pleiadians. It was constructed of a material which was like a phosphorescent ivory—it was both hard and translucent at the same time. The building blocks contained layers of delicate carvings, elaborate carvings within carvings. The hotel cast a luminous glow far into the sky.

Marduk liked to be alone these days. There just wasn't anyone even remotely interesting left out there. Really, when he got right down to it, most people or creatures were so damn boring and predictable. What did they know? *Nothing.* Marduk had convinced himself that he knew everything, and he had no one to talk to.

Lately, Marduk had been very irritable. There must be some amusement or diversion he hadn't already tried. Just then an awful thought crossed his mind: Could it be that he, Marduk himself, was in some way being affected by that imaginary *Wall* thing his ridiculous relatives were so worried about? Was it conceivable that Marduk's evolution, and therefore his ability to expand his personal enjoyment, had been frozen along with theirs, as they alleged?

Truly he was finding it harder and harder to have any fun at all. He expected to be amused by the installation of electronic media all across the planet Earth. Mass media from one central source would facilitate the transmission of propaganda and tighten the *Trap* that ensnared Earth's population. That would be fun, wouldn't it? Surely that was something to look forward to.

Marduk slumped on his golden throne. It was too bad, he thought, that women, including his wife, didn't amuse him. In fact, he didn't like women at all—except for his mother, just a little, because she had begged for his release from the pyramid when that shrew Inanna had plotted to kill him. Marduk didn't really even enjoy sex anymore—because, well, who would he want to have it with? No one interested him. No one attracted him. And with all of his armies of clones so splendidly duplicating his perfect brilliance and beauty, he didn't need to go on having children. Why bother?

Why bother? Lately, that dour thought increasingly came to mind. There were still a few activities that engaged his attention for short periods of time—a little drought here, a famine there, a nice plague, genocide (one of his favorites), and, of course, endless wars. But the depressing thought remained—Marduk was completely, utterly bored.

The droughts in the Land of the Ellipse began to occur on a regular basis and became insufferable. Anu, in his final incarnation in Filled-with-Stars' lineage, telepathically sent out a message to all the towns and villages across the land. Everyone was asked to meet in the caves and kivas, where Id and the Old Serpent Woman would appear to them simultaneously.

The call went out across 130,000 square miles of red and purple sandstone, shale, and limestone. Through the willows and the piñon trees, down the canyon walls, echoing across the singing waters, a clear sweet voice was heard in the heart and mind of each member of the tribe. Dropping their chisels, hoes, and baskets of grain, men, women, and children alike began to walk to the sacred kivas and caves in their village. They moved in silence, with only the sound of the wind to accompany them.

Once the tribal members had gathered in their sanctuaries, the Old Serpent Woman and the Dragon Princess Id appeared to them.

"The time has come," the Old Serpent Woman solemnly began. "Your adventure in this place has completed itself. The cycles of apparent life are ever in motion, and nothing remains unchanged. You have been faithful to this land, honoring nature as your own mother. Now the time has come for you to move on to a new home. The force of nature herself, as powerful waves of subtle vibrational frequencies, will carry you into a new dimension."

The Children of Anu trusted the Old Serpent Woman completely. For hundreds of years, they and their forebears had listened to her and relied on her wisdom to guide them. That which had been foretold had now come to pass, and they were not afraid. They were simply moving on to a new life. They felt elated and excited.

"You must hold in your hearts and minds," Id said, "the most exquisite, intense memories of your experiences of nature in this place. Focus with all of your being on *feeling* a perfect union with the sky, the trees, the cliffs, and the singing waters here in your land. Powerful feelings can stop time. Feeling those memories will bring you out of this time and into another world, a new life."

Then the Old Serpent Woman and Id began to chant a song of such sweet, haunting beauty as had never been heard before. One by one, each member of the tribe joined in the chant. The pure sounds resonating from them accelerated the spin of the atoms in their bodies, and thus the frequency of their cellular structure was increased. Invoking their cellular memory of nature's harmonious perfection, the Children of Anu became one with nature and her powerful wave oscillations, which in turned fueled their conscious focus and allowed them to let go of third dimensional reality.

Time, as measured by the heartbeat of the physical body, was suspended. All became lighter, transparent, weightless. The entire tribe began to fade into the hot desert air—thousands of the inhabitants of the Land of the Ellipse, the children of the Children of Anu, vanished into a higher dimensional world.

Over a campfire breakfast, Michael was busy explaining to Wolfie, Gracie, and Clarissa some of the great mysteries surrounding the canyon. One of the most perplexing of all the unexplained phenomena was a puzzling lack of bones.

"Compared to the number of dwellings, baskets, and pots that were found in all the diggings," Michael said, "practically no bones were discovered. Where did the tribe bury its dead? Why, with so much evidence of a large, thriving culture, were there so few skeletons? No one seems to know the answer."

Michael, finishing off his fourth biscuit, thought it was

wonderful that no one knew. He personally found comfort in the knowledge that not all questions could be answered, at least not in this world.

Far away in another dimension, Jehran turned to Inanna and said, "My beloved, we are nearing my homeland. Do you wish to remain in a state of pure thought, or would you like to become your lovely blue self once more?"

Inanna was just getting used to being without her body.

"Can I go back and forth between the two?" she asked with childlike delight.

"Why, of course!" Jehran answered, laughing.

"Well, all right then—I'll recreate my body now," Inanna said.

"Your body will be different in this dimensional reality," Jehran said. "It must adjust to the variation in frequency, and it will feel somehow lighter and more translucent. However, you will still be perfectly beautiful."

As the two lovers emerged into physical forms once again, Jehran embraced her.

"Thank you," Inanna said shyly; well, shyly for her.

The ship materialized around them and docked in a landing portal. The door opened to a party of beings who obviously had been eagerly awaiting the couple's arrival.

Jehran walked out to greet a very handsome, tall man with eyes like lightning and golden brown skin.

"Inanna, I want you to meet my oldest, closest friend. His name is Filled-with-Stars."

IX

CONVERSATIONS

A few self-chosen members of the tribe had always known that when the time came for the *shift*, they would remain in the desert southwest. Id had foretold of the coming of the white man from across the sea, and those of the Children of Anu who had decided to stay knew the grave dangers that lay before them. They saw in the Eye of the Mind that the Indian culture so sacred to them would be brutally destroyed.

A few brave individuals had prepared themselves to migrate into other tribes, and to teach them the ways of the Land of the Ellipse. They would serve as living examples for the others.

For all time, those who ventured into the canyons, kivas, and caves would see the symbols given by Anu and carved into stone, and they would remember. The desolate ruins on the plateau would forever endure as a monument to all of those who had once lived peacefully there. Standing in the shadows of what had been a thriving village, visitors would feel the tribe's presence and hear the soft shuffling of feet, the grinding of grain, and the wind as it whispered echoes of the past. And they would remember: Man once lived in harmony with the Earth.

As Inanna shook hands with Filled-with-Stars, she realized that this handsome man reminded her of someone she knew and loved. How could it be that Jehran's oldest friend would so closely resemble...yes, Filled-with-Stars looked very much like her great-grandfather Anu!

Filled-with-Stars sensed Inanna's curiosity and confusion. "I am one of Anu's multidimensional selves," he said warmly.

Inanna turned to Jehran.

"As you know, my love," Jehran said, "time does not exist, except as thought based on the vital rhythms of the body. In this dimension we are outside of time as you have experienced it before. In this layer of reality, *place* is an immediate consequence of consciousness.

"Filled-with-Stars and the other members of his tribe came here after they vanished from their earthly home, the Land of the Ellipse. When they attained the vibrational frequency of this dimension, they began to share our consciousness and so came to live with us."

Jehran continued, "Here in this layer of all-the-possible worlds, we exist beyond the denser wave lengths of time and space that you have known."

"Is that why we became thought?" Inanna asked.

"Yes. Our bodies, as they were, could not pass through the envelope of your universe into mine. Even fourth or fifth dimensional density will not pass through what might be called the *black hole* that separates the layers between each universe."

"But now that we are here, we can recreate our bodily forms..." Inanna was thinking out loud, ignoring Filled-with-Stars and the others.

"Yes, but you will notice you are somewhat changed." Jehran interrupted her self-absorption.

Inanna looked around her. Yes, everything was a little different—somehow lighter, brighter, the colors more intense.

The landing party walked from the port across an elevated bridge into a city built of luminous stone. Every building was round in shape; once inside, Inanna felt as if she were inside an ancient clay pot. The feeling was very soothing to her.

As soon as she regained her bearings, the very curious Inanna began to ask Filled-with-Stars questions about his relationship to Anu. She told Filled-with-Stars that her name, in fact, meant "beloved of Anu," and that her great-grandfather had always been good to her, loving her through even her most difficult times.

Filled-with-Stars was happy to share the story of his people and the Land of the Ellipse with Inanna. He told her that he had seen Anu only in dreams and visions; but perhaps someday Anu would come here, to Jehran's dimension.

As he finished his story, Filled-with-Stars nodded to his friend and then said to Inanna, "I can easily understand why both Anu and Jehran would love such a high-spirited lady as yourself."

Inanna was very pleased by such praise from Jehran's friend.

The group entered a comfortable room with big cozy chairs and a table laid with delicious food and wine. Inanna snuggled down into an oversized armchair, and Jehran sat beside her. They were both a little weary from their journey; some dinner and spirits were just what they needed.

In a relaxed atmosphere, they all felt as if they had known each other forever—which, in fact, they had.

After dinner, Filled-with-Stars once again spoke with Inanna.

"Do you know that one of your multidimensional selves is on a journey in the Land of the Ellipse?" he asked. "We have been watching through the *seeing-stones*. Observing those who visit our ancient home brings us joy, for the great plateau imbues those who venture there with our consciousness."

"That would have to be Gracie," Inanna said. "Take us to these *seeing-stones* so we may observe what she and her friends are up to."

In her travels through time and space, a part of Inanna's consciousness had been monitoring Gracie. Now, as she walked with Filled-with-Stars and Jehran toward the place where the *seeing-stones* were, Inanna accessed the latest data on her multidimensional self and friend.

In a way, she thought, *if it weren't for Gracie, I would not be here now with Jehran. Perhaps I can now help little Gracie once again.*

Filled-with-Stars, Jehran, and Inanna sat together in the kiva, a circular stone pit. In the center of the kiva were large blue crystals, surrounded by turquoise animal carvings and smooth purple sandstones. Inanna's eyes lit up when she saw the arrangement. Jehran lovingly touched her graceful blue hands, and the three began to focus on the *seeing-stones*. An oval opened up, displaying the hologram of an earthly desert landscape before them.

※

Clarissa, Michael, and Wolfie were relaxing around the campfire eating dried figs and pistachio nuts. Dancing flames reflected gently across their faces on this perfectly clear night. The air in this place was so clean that when they breathed, they felt as though they were drinking fresh spring water from a mountain aquifer.

Gracie stood up, stretched, and then quietly wandered off by herself; she wanted to be alone to meditate under the thick canopy of stars. She found a large rock halfway up the cliffs to sit and meditate on. The climb was not too arduous, and the surface of the rock was smooth. Sitting under the silent stars, Gracie called out to Thel Dar and Inanna. What more could she do before the transformational shift—when the world as she knew it would split itself into two or more worlds of consciousness?

In her heart, Gracie knew that the future depended solely on each individual, for each one alone possessed the power to align with a dimensional frequency. Still, she wanted to help, were it possible. Allowing herself to be carried into the beauty of the sky above her, Gracie remembered her solitary nights on Lost Mountain. She had changed on that mountain, and her life was still changing; she had given up wondering where it would all lead. She had learned to listen and trust in that special knowingness she felt within her. A small part of her was already in harmony with the Creator of this starry sky, and that was all she needed to lead her forward into the next moment of time.

Gracie knew she didn't want to "teach" anybody anything, ever. Experience had shown her that "teachers" became tyrants sooner or later. Once a truth became a dogma, it ceased to be truth. Everyone contained the truth within herself or himself, and discovering it was life's adventure. All Gracie could do was listen to the divine presence within her, and allow the feeling to flow out to others as a force of Prime Creator's Love.

Gracie realized she had received her answer. Was there more she could do? No, just be; that was all that was required of her. She felt a sweet serenity as she slowly clambered down from the rock to return to the campfire and her friends.

Michael was discussing alien landings as usual; he was filling Wolfie in on all the relevant facts.

"Statistics estimate that an average of more than 3,000 close encounters occur every twenty-four hours in the United States alone. Imagine what must be going on worldwide, and in remote areas where the people rarely have any way to report these occurrences."

Gracie sat down next to Wolfie; he put his arm around her and hugged her. "Are you cold?" he asked.

"No, thank you, I'm fine."

But Clarissa, thinking about what Michael was saying, shivered. "Gee, all this talk of alien abductions and stuff scares me."

Gracie smiled at her. "When I was a teenager," she said, "I painted a series of pictures of the ones with the big black eyes. It was way before that book or the movie came out, and I had never seen any depictions of them. When I saw the famous book cover, I was shocked. I had always wondered who, or what, my paintings were."

Michael whistled softly. "No kidding?"

"Yes," Gracie said. "The amazing thing was that people I knew actually *liked* the paintings. Everyone wanted them, even though they were weird. People bought them, only to have them stolen. It was strange. The paintings must have connected with people's subconscious memories. Every single painting was eventually stolen, and all I have left is one photograph."

"Wow!" Michael said. "It sounds like you must have been abducted."

"Maybe, but I don't remember it. And strangely, whenever I see them portrayed, I always like the little Greys with their big eyes. In fact, I always think of them as being innocent, like children.

"For a time, I lived on a mountain by myself, and at first I was fearful. I had some visions that made me apprehensive. Later, I experienced powerful feelings I can't even begin to describe, and I came to realize that everything—including scary little aliens—was a part of God's creation. Prime Creator made everything, and *was* everything. Even the creatures which frighten us come from the matrix of God.

"One night Inanna and I, together, began to rise into a state of *knowing*. We *knew* that everything was God. We *knew* that even the tyrants were God, and we felt love for them as such. However misguided they were, they too formed a part of creation. That new understanding easily set us free from them."

Clarissa murmured, "That's called loving your enemies, isn't it."

187

"Yes, I think so." Gracie was smiling. "Something like turning the other cheek, knowing that the Spirit that lives within you can never be destroyed. You can be altered in form temporarily, unpleasantly changed, as it were; but the *within* never dies. So who can really harm you?

"It is our fear that most harms us. We allow fear to consume us, and we forget that this is a dance, a cosmic game in the most profound sense. This reality consists of coordinates in the time-space continuum, placed here by Prime Creator so that we may experience duality. Once we remember that we are a part of the Creator's eternal play, fear ceases to exist."

The fire was dying down and the stars covered the dark sky above them. Everyone was silent as they listened to the stillness in the night.

X

THE DEAL

Over the centuries, Marduk wrapped himself in numerous names and faces. His varied expressions of tyranny mirrored the collective fears of the humans he controlled. A master of disguises, Marduk fooled his victims over and over, appearing in new and altered forms; but snake oil is snake oil, by any other name.

Marduk was well aware that time flowed in cycles and was divided into four ages. The fourth cycle, the Age of Conflict or the Kali Yuga, was Marduk's favorite.

As humankind progressed into this age and continued its fall into the lower vibrational frequencies, people lost their ability to remember—and without the gift of memory, humans increasingly relied on writing for the transmission of knowledge. To be considered credible a historical event had to be written on clay, papyrus, or paper and recorded by a recognized authority. That "authority" inevitably had his benefactor's best interests in mind.

This turn of events made Marduk's job so much easier. The human species no longer remembered a time on Earth when the tyrants didn't rule; they grew to accept tyranny as the norm. Having no written evidence of any other reality, they came to believe they had committed some original sin, and were thus destined to live in fear and conflict.

No one remembered where he or she came from, or that access to Prime Creator lay dormant within everyone. The truth was veiled by the frequencies of a third dimensional illusion. Such ignorance gave Marduk free range for his deviant mind to play. The descent of the human race accelerated as the Kali Yuga progressed.

People had come to pursue false values. Greed replaced integrity, and families fell apart as men and women devoted themselves to the acquisition of money. The numbers of abandoned children increased; in some places children, alone and unprotected, were hunted down in the streets and killed.

The rulers of state began to appropriate more and more wealth through taxation. Criminal behavior among elected officials, who often had no moral code beyond self-aggrandizement, was accepted.

The land and the waters became increasingly poisoned. Sea animals began to die in large numbers, their immune systems weakened by an ocean of toxins. Famine became commonplace and plagues began.

No one trusted anyone. Lawsuits replaced the handshake, and everyone was consumed with envy.

Looking out on a job well done, Marduk was pleased; the Kali Yuga allowed him to fulfill his destiny.

In the 1930s, Marduk found a man living in Western Europe who had "his" kind of potential. This man had an enormous reservoir of stifled energy. Thoroughly convinced of his own genius, he was sure it was his destiny to become a great artist; however, this potent delusion was thwarted by an observable lack of talent. An inherent flaw in his character—a peculiar weakness in the control of his own will, combined with an insatiable need for attention—made this unknown failure eminently vulnerable to Marduk's control.

Marduk inserted visions of an exalted destiny into the dreams of this weak soul, visions of marching armies and cheering crowds all hailing the "Fuehrer." Scenes of war—momentous victories, conquered cities, and death camps—puffed up the little man's ego, and led him to believe that he was predestined to rule the world. Fate had marked him as the Fuehrer for the task of "purifying" the human race. Destiny called him, via Marduk's tricks.

In a short time, Marduk managed to turn this nobody—a failed impressionist painter—into the infamous Fuehrer, a charismatic and ruthless tyrant who hypnotized and devastated the world with his madness. Invading peaceful countries, slaughtering innocent people, the Fuehrer became the most feared and hated man on the Earth.

The countries that had not yet been invaded aligned themselves to defend what remained of the free world. Millions of lives had already been lost; what was needed now was a magic weapon—a weapon terrible enough to crush this merciless tyrant. Brilliant scientists worked frantically in a worldwide effort to devise such a weapon.

Desperation, as always, brought opportunities to Lord

Marduk. The supposed Law of Non-Interference had been an annoyance to him, not that he had obeyed it or any such ridiculous thing. It would be amusing to flout it flagrantly and outwit those nuisance Etherians. From his control room on Nibiru, Marduk conceived a plan to strike a deal with the desperate scientists.

The deal was offered by a handful of Marduk's clones dressed in black business suits. The men in black introduced themselves as technologically advanced aliens from a distant planet, and they offered the scientists the mathematical formulas required to create a weapon of greater destructive power than any known to man. In return, the scientists were to agree to let the aliens abduct human beings for the purpose of extracting their DNA.

At first the scientists were outraged and refused; the deal smacked of soul-selling, or at least of trafficking in body parts. Splintering into factions, they argued among themselves; some wanted the technology at any cost, others were willing to compromise. In the end the scientists accepted the deal, but demanded certain guarantees.

What exactly would happen to those who were abducted?

The men in black made promises: The abductees would be returned to their normal lives, any memories of the experience would be erased, and, except for the occasional unexplained scar, their lives would continue unaffected.

The scientists allowed themselves to be comforted by these assurances. Surely it was far more important to win the war, and thus save thousands of lives, than to be overly concerned with the fate of a few humans who wouldn't remember anything anyway.

Think of all the progress that might be made, the new

leaps in scientific understanding, they argued. Who knew what these mathematical formulas might lead to? Why, one day they might prove to be the key to a world without hunger and suffering; perhaps the formulas could eliminate disease and even aging itself. Like all humans, the scientists got carried away by their personal dreams of success, glory, and power.

So the deal was struck. A small secret group of elite scientists and a cadre of high-ranking military men agreed to allow the abduction of a limited number of human beings. In return, Marduk's clones gave them the previously unknown and entirely astonishing mathematical formulas.

The scientists went to work with the magic math, and the abductions began.

Lord Marduk had managed to acquire permission to interfere with the human race from the humans themselves. He had circumvented the Law of Non-Interference, and amused himself by outwitting the Etherians.

Marduk had many uses for the DNA; he could enhance his clones, and he could sell it to other extraterrestrials in return for mercenaries. What made the human DNA so attractive to alien races was that it contained the biochemical sequencing for the capacity to feel; because feelings are the power that transduces thought into reality, they are essential to the creative process. An array of alien races from all over the Galaxy eagerly lined up to purchase human DNA.

In the beginning, Marduk assumed he could control the DNA trade. But as in many lucrative markets, ingenious pirates soon stepped in to take their cut. By the 1950s, unidentified flying objects were sighted all over the planet.

Meanwhile, the scientists made progress; they finally

produced the weapon they coveted, and it did seemingly help to end the war—at a great cost of life, as usual.

After the war, the number of abductions increased dramatically. Moreover, the "guarantees" the aliens had promised were not holding, and bewildered abductees began to remember what had happened to them. Some of those who knew about the deal threatened to tell the truth; but one way or another, they were discredited or silenced.

The military cadre was forced to devise a large-scale cover-up, and created a systematic procedure for debunking all reports of UFOs and alien abductions. The procedure was simple: The authorities first confirmed the sightings and then categorically denied them, effectively confusing the hell out of anyone naive enough to report them. The authorities found it easy, for awhile, to make people doubt what they had actually seen.

Even so, reports of UFO sightings and strange stories of bizarre abductions grew at an alarming rate. The truth was leaking out.

The scientists and the military had lost control of their deal, and Marduk had lost his monopoly on the trade of DNA. Diverse alien races were making clandestine offers of their technologies to governments and covert groups all over the planet in return for human and animal DNA. The deal was completely out of control.

From the Mother Ship, the Etherians continued to monitor Marduk's escapades and the progress of the human race. The hope remained that the inhabitants of planet Earth would soon evolve forward into a state of wisdom, and *remember* who they were.

XI

SWAMP FIRES

Clarissa had wandered off alone to think. She needed some time to assimilate what she had experienced in this magical place. As much as she loved Michael, at times she wanted to be apart from him for a little while.

Michael often reminded Clarissa of her father. The realization annoyed her—it seemed so predictable. How often did women fall in love with guys just like their fathers, or worse, attempt to escape the whole syndrome by falling for their fathers' polar opposites?

Clarissa's father had been quite a character indeed, a wild and impulsive, highly creative individual who had lived from moment to moment. Will, short for William, had been born in the hills of northern Scotland just before World War II. His father went off to serve in the army and left Will's mother to raise two young sons alone. Will dreamed of joining his father in combat. He roamed the nearby hills and perched on craggy rocks, picturing vivid battle scenes in his mind. In Will's imagination, he and his father fought valiantly side by side. Will became an excellent rock climber at an early age; climbing took his mind off his father's absence and his mother's innumerable anxieties.

When Will's father returned home to his family after the war, he was a broken man, not at all the hero Will had frequently imagined him to be. His nerves were shot. He spent the remaining years of his life sitting at the kitchen table, sipping beer and silently smoking cigarettes one after the other, his nicotine-stained fingers trembling.

Will was appalled; this shell of a man wasn't even remotely like the father he had dreamed of. Where was the brave warrior he had fought beside so many times in his imagination?

After his father's death, Will suppressed his grief and anger by climbing mountains. As soon as he finished college, Will followed his "mates" to the Alps. He and his friends were hard-living, hard-drinking young climbers who lived for the adrenaline rush of defying death.

Will was a smooth talker with a handsome, craggy face and curly blonde hair. The girls in the local bars idolized Will and his friends as heroes; these young men were seen as brave, exciting adventurers, who drank all night, made love and left before dawn for their mountains. In the kind of romantic world which belongs only to the young, Will was acting out the courage he had imagined his father possessed.

In the bars of Zermatt, certain newly discovered mind-expanding drugs were being passed around. Will and his buddies naturally jumped at the chance of more adventure, more adrenaline rushes. In those early days of experimentation, no one knew the long-term results of taking such chemical compounds. Will and his mountain climbing gang were, by their own choice, the unknowing guinea pigs for a new frontier.

There were pills to keep them up so they could climb all day and drink all night, and there were pills to take when they made love or reached the top of the mountain. Still other pills took them to altered states of consciousness, mysterious dimensional worlds, and even allowed them to feel, however temporarily, that they were one with the entire Universe.

Inevitably, this reckless game began to take its toll on the climbers' nerves, courage, and health. One by one, Will's friends began to die; some were buried in avalanches, some fell off the mountain in freak accidents, and others simply "burned out." As for Will, he lost his nerve; one day, fear overcame his reason and he knew he could never climb again.

Will had begun to drink in earnest by the time he met Clarissa's mother some years later. She was much younger than Will and an innocent dreamer. Falling in love with Will's romantic past, she idealized his lost climbing days, believing she could rescue him from the drink.

Clarissa had been a surprise to them both, but not even the birth of a child could stop Will from his downward spiral. Like many in his generation, he believed in hallucinogens; Will combined drugs and alcohol with lethal results. He wouldn't listen to anyone and he wouldn't ask for help.

Clarissa's mother tried everything to hold on to Will. She even left him a few times, only to run back; they lived together off and on. He wasn't mean to her or Clarissa, merely self-destructive and pathetic. Even though she couldn't stop loving him, Clarissa's mother knew that eventually she would have to leave him to protect the child and save herself.

Clarissa was still so young when she last saw her father that Will was only a memory for her now—the bittersweet stories of the once brave and handsome youth who climbed the great mountains of stone and ice.

Like her father, Michael was a risk taker. Bravely determined to learn the truth at any cost, Michael was prepared to climb dark icy walls in his consciousness and tear away the veils of ignorance. He had inherited the legacy of Will's generation, a legacy of both hope and destruction. Perhaps throughout time there had always been courageous souls who ventured into the unknown, only to end up as casualties.

Whenever Clarissa remembered her father and her childhood, she pictured swamp fires. In all that pain, buried somewhere deep in the murky anguish, lay her source of strength. Clarissa was determined to have her father's courage; but, unlike him, she would not be a victim. Clearly, the only way to move forward in this life was to walk on what she understood as "the razor's edge."

Sitting alone in the Land of the Ellipse, Clarissa began to cry. In her mind she pictured an old black-and-white photograph of her father. He was perched, seemingly virtually suspended, on the sheer vertical face of a rock cliff. As often as she had seen that photograph, she had not been able to imagine what his feet were standing on—he looked as if he were floating beside the cliff with his fingers dug into the rock. The sun lit his golden hair, and he was smiling arrogantly as if bursting from the pleasure of his achievement.

Powerful and confusing emotions welled up inside Clarissa; no matter how her father had failed her, she loved him.

Clarissa heard a voice inside her.

Hey, Love, don't cry.

There before her, floating in the air as the young man in the photograph, was her father, Will.

Clarissa, please don't cry. I came into this world to learn, and learn I did through my life's experience. I love you, my girl. Perhaps one day you may find me cradled in your arms as a newborn babe.

Clarissa wept uncontrollably; her nose was running and she fumbled in her backpack for a tissue. Trying to get her emotions under control, she thought, *Damn swamp fires! I'm always putting out swamp fires.*

She looked up, but her father was gone. His words hung in the air: "...find me cradled in your arms as a newborn babe."

XII

THE VISIT

Filled-with-Stars, Jehran, and Inanna looked up from the *seeing-stones*. The oval remained there before them, opening up a view of the Land of the Ellipse on the planet Earth, which was to all appearances far away. The idea of visiting Gracie, Wolfie, Clarissa, and Michael in their desert camp occurred simultaneously to all three of them.

Inanna said excitedly, "Let's form a magnificent spaceship for them. Clarissa's Michael loves UFO mysteries, and I'm sure such a vehicle would amuse Herr Mozart. Also, I think we should arrange to invite Anu." She turned to Filled-with-Stars. "What do you think?"

"I would be so pleased to be with Anu, and perhaps Id, in my ancient homeland." The light of happy memories sparkled in Filled-with-Stars' eyes.

Jehran thought, *Perhaps I will create an etheric harpsichord for Wolfie to play upon in these desert cliffs.*

"Oh, that's a good idea, Jehran," Inanna blurted out, reading her lover's thoughts. "I would love to hear Mozart play in the desert canyons. And how I miss Anu; it will be wonderful to see him. I want you to meet him; I know you two will like each other."

"Well, of course, since we both love you, my darling." Jehran gave Inanna a little kiss.

And so there was a gathering in the Land of the Ellipse, an implausible and fantastic meeting of friends who, throughout non-existent time, dearly loved each other.

Clarissa had returned to the little group; she and her companions sat around a small fire heating a can of organically grown baked beans. Wolfie was eating graham crackers with Gracie's dog Bear, and Michael was cutting up oranges and apples for a nice salad.

Suddenly a golden disk appeared high in the sky above them. Shining brightly in the light of day, it hovered for a few moments and then slowly lowered itself closer to them. They could see its splendid design; blue lights encircled the bottom of the ship and emitted blue rays onto the ground.

Windows around the top of the disk appeared opaque one moment and transparent the next. The ship seemed to be made of pure gold, and it was decorated with a very simple, elegant design, the patterns of which reflected the harmonic calculations of the ship's structural physics; that was Inanna's idea.

As the ship landed, a soft mist surrounded it; a door

opened silently. Inanna, Jehran, Anu, Filled-with-Stars, and Moonwaters descended onto a huge purple sandstone.

Gracie and Clarissa recognized Inanna at once, and Wolfie knew Jehran. Michael was beside himself with excitement. He imagined himself boarding the ship with the visitors and flying away; surely, Clarissa would want to come too.

Filled-with-Stars was delighted to be in his homeland. Taking Moonwaters' hand in his, he looked up at the caves in the cliffs and down to the stream running through his canyon. Life had been good here. He remembered the sound of children's laughter, the soft murmurings of his tribe as they went about their daily lives. A hawk flew across the clear blue sky above him, and Filled-with-Stars felt a tear run down his cheek.

Deep in the forever Void, Thel Dar and Tathata delighted in observing the many aspects of themselves playing in the layers of potential realities in all-the-possible worlds. From within the Mind of God, the two companions whirled together in pulsating, thunderous joy—and filled the limitless darkness with supra-luminal force, because they could.

In the Land of the Ellipse, everyone had gathered in the ruins of an old kiva. Anu began to speak.

"It was my wish to create a race of beings who would serve to balance the mischief we had brought to this planet and to the race of human beings living here. That wish was fulfilled beyond my dreams with the help of the wisdom of the Dragon Princess, Id."

At this, Anu gestured toward the hallowed center of the kiva, the *sipapu*, and from this sacred opening Id emerged. She had joined them from the ancient secret tunnel which led to Inner Earth. Id was dressed in a luminous golden gown; her favorite blood rubies covered her throat and arms.

The sun was setting, and Wolfie lit a small fire as Id began to speak.

"The clans of the Dragon and Snake," Id said, "have always known that there is no deep reality, and thus no reason to cling to temporary illusions. The world we see around us appears real enough, but its forms float upon another world, which we dragons call the invisible or *unreal* world.

"The invisible world comprises the potential for infinite varieties of existence. An illimitable number of unrealized tendencies interact with the consciousness of the watcher observing it. The invisible world is the underlying matrix and source of all probabilities in the visible world.

"The watcher creates a reality by fusing his or her consciousness with that reality through focus, and thus fueling it. There is no separation between the watcher and its reality; they are one and the same. As a watcher shifts focus from one part of the invisible matrix world to another, realities appear as multi-layered films, each layer reflecting the unique consciousness of the watcher who observes it.

"Therefore, there are as many versions of a perceived reality as there are levels of consciousness. Whoever has come to the Land of the Ellipse has simply seen whatever was reflected from within their own vibrational frequency."

Anu added, "When the tyrants' conquistadors came to

overrun this land, they saw only the remains of a poor and wretched civilization. Their hearts could not imagine men and women who valued something greater than gold."

Id continued, "Those who came here with pure hearts seeking hope for the human race saw only what Anu had intended them to see. The rocks held the memory of the tribe's consciousness. For those who could truly see and listen, the shadows and sounds revealed an ancient people truly advanced in understanding. The Children of Anu did not measure their wealth in gold.

"Those who came here in fear saw their own fears reflected back to them. In the shadows of the canyons, and in abandoned caves, they envisioned the ghosts of famine and the flesh-eating demons of death. Layers of realities built up in this magical place to teach all who came. .

"And all the while," Id concluded, "the Children of Anu were safe in a place of peace that resonated with their own being—Jehran's home. At a certain point in evolution, location becomes a matter of consciousness. Where you are is a matter of what you think, and what you *know*."

The fire burned softly in the circular stone kiva. Michael put his arm around Clarissa; perhaps he didn't need to jump into a spaceship and fly off just yet. Perhaps, he thought, there was more life to be lived right here, with the woman he loved, on the good old planet Earth. He understood that eventually he could go, in consciousness, anywhere he liked, if only he allowed himself to do so. Opening up the rest of his brain was his God-given right; the secret was locked somewhere in his latent DNA, and Michael now knew that he would be able to find the key.

What was his hurry? In the meantime, why not just love his beautiful Clarissa? Maybe now would be a good time to make babies together. He had never felt ready before today; but for some reason, the idea now filled him with anticipation.

✳

After Wolfie gave a fine performance of his music on the harpsichord Jehran had brought along, everyone retired to the kiva and was pleasantly napping in front of the cozy fire, except Inanna and Anu. The two talked quietly together. Anu wanted to assure himself that his great-grand-daughter was happy.

He spoke softly so the others would not hear. "And so, my beloved girl, how does life find you?"

"So much has happened since the meeting of the Inter-Galactic Council in the Great Hall," said Inanna. "I could never have predicted any of this. Now I see clearly that tyranny is a limited and limiting form of expression. Why would anyone want to control another, when it is so much more interesting to interact with those who can freely express their own unique souls? I was bored before, Anu, really bored."

"As was I, my darling girl. No one can stay the same forever and not become bored. Even Marduk must eventually change. Imagine how weary he must be—having only clones of himself to talk to, or those poor wretched beings who live in continual fear of his wrath. Marduk may control and manipulate his world, but a life without love, ruled by fear, must become barren and empty."

"Yes," Inanna laughed. "Sometimes I imagine my cousin Marduk surrounded by all his lackeys and palaces, bored by it all and irritable as he vainly attempts to amuse himself."

Anu grinned wryly at the thought. "Most of our family has evolved, and we will soon be moving on to higher dimensional worlds and fresh possibilities. I only want to know that you are happy with this Jehran fellow, and that he will be good to you. You know that I love you, my Inanna. Your well-being is of the greatest concern to me."

Out of the corner of her eye, Inanna could see that Jehran was not really asleep, but only politely pretending to be, so that she and Anu could talk.

"Yes, Anu, I am happy. Jehran is the kindest man I have ever known; his integrity and gentle intelligence are an inspiration to me. I really do love him."

Anu smiled. "Ah, that is good, little one! Perhaps someday you may come to me with children to bounce upon my knee?"

Inanna blushed. "Anu, I don't know what to say."

"Ha! My Inanna, at a loss for words!" Anu was laughing heartily now and waking everyone up. "Well, how things have changed!"

On the top floor of a towering skyscraper in a dark and polluted city, Marduk sat hunched miserably in front of his monitors.

Damn them, he thought. *I know they're down there somewhere; I can even hear them, feel them. They're talking about me.*

Marduk pushed one of 10,000 buttons, and an android clone entered the control room.

"Yes, great master. How may I serve you?" The clone inquired.

"You jackass, is this all the power you can get me?

Something's wrong with my satellite monitoring systems. You idiots have miscalculated again! I won't stand for this! Get me more power, or someone will be punished!"

The android clone fell to his knees, as he had been programmed to do, saying, "Oh, great master. How may I serve you?"

Marduk kicked the android violently. Its circuitry altered by the blow, it began to repeat, "Oh, may I great you, serve master? Great serve, may oh! You may serve, oh great, may oh!"

Marduk was appalled. He was already annoyed, and now this imbecile android was tormenting him with mean-ingless gibberish. How, he fumed, was it possible that his technology was too weak to espy the members of his family, who were obviously infesting the Land of the Ellipse? Could it be that there were frequencies he could not perceive, even with all of his power and wealth? Bloody nuisance—some of his exasperating relatives were down there; he knew that. *Damn!* For the life of him, Marduk just could not see them.

Safe in the kiva, the little party enjoyed a fine time. Inanna had brought a picnic dinner with delicious foods and wonderful wines from all over the galaxy. She had even remembered to bring some chocolates from Valthezon. Glasses in hand, the friends toasted to each other and the grandness of life.

"To Prime Creator!" Their voices rang out into the desert night and up through the stars, far into the forever Void.

XIII

MUTATION
AND COMPASSION

The gathering of friends in the Land of the Ellipse, after an enjoyable meal, turned their attention to Filled-with-Stars, who began to speak. His heart overflowed with loving memories of his people, the tribe, the Children of Anu, who had once thrived in this magical place. As he expressed his love for Mother Earth, his etheric body became more solid—as if the very force of loving this land compelled him toward materialization.

As he stood before them, the firelight reflected off his muscled golden-brown body, and his sky-blue eyes burned with starlight. Harmony with life, and his own integrity, flowed from him as a gentle magnetic presence. As Filled-with-Stars spoke, Anu felt a deep affection for his first multidimensional self.

"After we passed from this dimensional plane," Filled-with-Stars explained, "we became known as the Ancient Ones. From the place beyond the rainbow, we came to those who called out to us in times of need, and throughout these many years we have uplifted lost and lonely souls. Many tribes on this continent and beyond were given access to higher dimensional frequencies by those they called the *Ancient Ones*.

"A shift is coming for planet Earth, and the veils that have hidden the other dimensional worlds from human sight are about to lift. For those who have the courage to open their minds to the *vision of the heart*, those dimensions will once again be open to their sight, as they were eons ago.

"Ignorance of all-the-possible worlds will disappear for those who desire such enlightenment. Seeing with the heart will lift them through illusion, and allow them to know the infinite vastness of the Mind of God. It will be a time of homecoming, of rejoicing in remembrance, for all who choose it.

"For those who, through their own will, have the courage to *know*, the veils will part and all-the-possible worlds will open to them."

As Gracie listened to Filled-with-Stars talk about courage, she remembered Thel Dar once saying that its name could be taken to mean "the courage to know." The word *thel* referred to will, and only a focused will could generate the kind of courage required to know what lay beyond the veils of ignorance. A radiant-light Being had no name; it was solely a frequency, and thus beyond name. Thel Dar had provided Gracie with the name in order that she might have a connecting sound to help her be brave.

In the stillness of the desert night, Filled-with-Stars and Moonwaters chanted a song of the Ancient Ones, and each soul in the kiva began to resonate with the long pure tones that flowed out in slow and haunting sequence. As the sound built force within them, the friends all felt an increasing sense of love: love for each other, love for the Earth, and love for God.

Even Wolfie, with all his guileless genius, found himself profoundly moved by the chant. Eventually everyone joined in, singing the ancient song as if it had always been familiar to them as the song of their soul.

The stones in the kiva, vibrating from the impact of familiar sounds, began to glow mysteriously with a soft blue light. As the sacred sounds entered the singers' physical bodies and acted upon their cells, the very DNA within those cells was altered by the increasing vibrational frequency.

Anu felt a wrenching change. As he released the last of his old habits of tyranny and control, a joyful bliss consumed him—and the momentum of that bliss created powerful waves which were felt on the orbiting satellite by Antu, Anu's beloved sister/wife, and their son, Enlil. Because Anu's DNA had been altered, all of the members of his family—along with the Anunnaki who were open to such a transformation—experienced a shift in their very being and became more conscious.

Id was likewise mutating in response to the sounds in the kiva. She directed her energies down into the Kingdoms of the Dragons and Snakes, and a feeling of upliftment floated into the laboratories of Ninhursag and Enki. This sister and brother, who had together altered the human DNA to create a race of workers, felt themselves change. As they were lifted into a higher state of consciousness, the two siblings easily transcended their differences and remembered they both had been born of the same source, the Mind of God. They realized that there was no point in holding onto archaic wounds and grudges at such a level of consciousness.

Inanna and Jehran likewise were transformed by the sounds of the Ancient Ones. The couple united with their friends in the kiva to radiate rapture across all-the-possible worlds, even beyond space and time. Wolfie and Gracie found new strength to become, by their very presence, unshakable beacons for others.

Michael and Clarissa began to remember who they were, just as Gracie had on Lost Mountain. As the frequencies of their DNA heightened, their thoughts changed simultaneously, mutating their bodies. The two lovers looked into each other's eyes, but did not need to speak; a new understanding had formed itself between them.

Clarissa had long dreamed of having a baby. Bringing children into the world is the highest expression of faith in the future; even the fiery Inanna had begun to imagine a chubby baby with big brown eyes and turquoise-blue skin running across cool floors of lapis-lazuli.

Inanna had opened the possibility of extraordinary experiences for Jehran, and now he too found himself thinking of children.

That night, all over the Earth, those who were lost and alone felt comforted somehow. Waves of love washed over countless hopeless souls and lifted their broken spirits. It was time to come home—time to *remember who they were.*

✳

Back in the kiva in the Land of the Ellipse, Anu broke
the perfect silence of that night.

"Someone is coming."

XIV

ENFOLDING SPACE

Alone in his private control room, Marduk monitored the southwestern high-desert sector of the North American continent on the planet Earth.

To his considerable annoyance, nothing appeared on the monitors. The blank monitors reflected the profound vacuity of his wearisome existence. Marduk was unspeakably bored. These days, everyone he came into contact with bored him. He felt listless, lethargic. He found it easier to spend his time alone than to be exasperated by tiresome, sniveling underlings or chattering android clones.

In an effort to bypass the monitors, Marduk tried to project all of his psychic powers into that puzzling canyon. But the Land of the Ellipse stayed invisible to him. Still, he knew they were down there somewhere. *Damn them!* he fumed, cursing his family.

Before his extensive detection surveillance had failed him, he had tracked one of Anu's ships to an area near the desert sector he now found closed to him. Worse, he had sensed that yet another, more imposing craft had disappeared into what could only be an Etherian cloaking fog. Realizing that he was powerless against the Etherians only served to further rile the Lord Marduk. Something unknown to him was deforming space itself around that desert area, as if the entire section had folded in on itself in order to elude his attention.

His failure to grasp this enigma, coupled with the gnawing suspicion that the solution might be beyond him, fueled his exasperation and made him bilious with acids; he could feel the beginnings of an ulcer in his reptilian gut. Day by day, the supplies of fear and despair were disappearing from the face of the Earth. What would he do if the source of his power continued to diminish at this rate? How would he support his armies if the humans—who under his ingenious guidance generated more than adequate quantities of fear—suddenly activated their latent DNA and remembered who they were? What would be left for Marduk as an insolvent tyrant? Such speculation was insufferable to his reptilian soul.

He thought, *I must find a way to circumvent this cloaking device and deal with this damnable Wave thing.* Finishing off the last sip of an eighteenth-century cognac, Marduk called in General Algol Benzene, leader of the Venomars, a crack reptilian stealth squadron.

That evening General Benzene, cloaked in black and golden robes, entered Lord Marduk's chambers. Algol felt no affection for his despot master, and being summoned to a personal audience riled him. As long as he could remember, he had wanted to assassinate Lord Marduk and take his place. Lately, observing that Marduk was losing his edge, Algol had begun to think that the time was right.

Marduk was accustomed to such rivalrous opposition; he did not mind what Benzene thought, as long as he remained in abject obedience.

"Algol, it is good to see you," Marduk lied.

"Master." Algol bowed appropriately.

Marduk pointed to a large electronic map. "I command you to take a squadron of our black Venomars to this desert in the southwestern sector of the North American continent. Destroy every living thing in this area."

"It is done, Master." Algol, his head bowed, saluted with a fist upon his considerable chest and backed obsequiously out of the control room.

Pathetic! thought Marduk. *Ah! And if he fails, I shall easily replace him.*

Marduk respected no one, not even General Algol Benzene. Marduk alone would do all of the thinking for his new world order. As of late, he had executed his plans for a worldwide merger of all of the media conglomerates on Earth. There would be only one source of information for the entire population of the planet. He would continue to numb what remained of the human brain into the shifting repetitions of fear and resentment. Relieved of the burden of thinking for themselves, the humans would again be confined to emitting abundant quantities of fear for the sustenance of Marduk's empire.

Deep into the night, Marduk brooded. His red eyes glowed in the dark control room as they stared vacantly into the light of the monitoring screens. *There must be something more I can do...*

✳

Inanna, Anu, and the others watched a familiar sight in the night sky. A spaceship, which Anu recognized at once as belonging to his son Enlil, gracefully drifted down to the rocky earth. The luminous ship pulsated with the purple and green lights encircling its perimeter. Upon landing, an opening appeared in the side of the ship and Enlil emerged with his mother, Antu. Behind them were four Etherians and the Lady of the Garnets with her gallant husband, the Commander.

Michael enthusiastically greeted his old friend.

"Commander, it's great to see you again. I want you to meet the woman I love, Clarissa."

As greetings were exchanged, Antu at once embraced Id in a gesture of genuine respect and friendship, and congratulated her on the work she had done in imparting vital wisdom to Anu's tribe. Their experiment in consciousness had brought honor to the entire family, and Antu was grateful to Id for her courage and her achievements. There was no trace of jealousy in Antu's demeanor, and Id recognized her sincerity at once.

Anu keenly observed that Enlil was ill at ease.

"My son, what vexes you?" he asked.

"Father, on our way here, I was hard-pressed to elude a squadron of Marduk's Venomars. I had not expected to be stalked so boldly, but I am sure the Etherian cloaking devices served us well."

"Here you need not be concerned, my son," Anu said calmly.

"So it is, Lord Anu," one of the Etherians said appreciatively. "We have been monitoring your encampment. The frequencies of this place have been well masked. Excellent work."

Inanna laughed mischievously. "It seems we are completely invisible to our cousin Marduk. Yet the Etherians have no trouble finding us!"

Anu privately reflected on the generosity of spirit with which Antu had greeted Id. As far as he could tell, the two women were quite comfortable being together, and really seemed to be enjoying themselves. Anu never knew what to expect from Antu, a quality which had always made him love her even more.

Meanwhile, Id was confiding in Antu, explaining that it was her love for her son, Enki, that had driven her to help ease the human condition. Id understood that Enki endured the terrible burden of knowing that he and Ninhursag were responsible for altering the human DNA. Id had wanted to take part in the healing for her son's sake, as well as for her own. She still hoped that one day Marduk, that misguided grandson of hers, might come to the end of his madness.

The night sky was resplendent with stars, and everyone was having a wonderful time. Inanna poured the wines. The Lady of the Garnets wanted to hear all about how Inanna was getting along with Jehran, so the two friends wandered up into the cliffs together.

The Commander, noticing Michael's fascination with Enlil's ship, offered to take Clarissa, Michael, Gracie, and Wolfie for a small tour.

Anu remained with Jehran, Enlil, and the Etherians for a genial conversation. Gracie's dog, Bear, who had taken an immediate liking to Anu, settled himself down at Anu's feet, which greatly amused and pleased the noble old man.

It was a time of communion among friends in the Land of the Ellipse.

XV

DESIRE

Deep in the forever Void, Thel Dar and Tathata looked into the heart of this intimate gathering of family and friends. Pleased by what they saw, the two radiant-light Beings allowed a sweet thought to form between them. Soon a new Earth would make itself known, as more and more expressions of Prime Creator chose to transcend the polarities and evolve beyond the modes of survival and fear.

Thel Dar spoke. "The veils will lift."

"Yes, the veils will lift and we will have some fun!" Tathata added, smiling.

The pleasing frequencies of this thought resonated through the Mind of God and attracted three familiar entities. Beyond time and space, the three appeared before Thel Dar and Tathata.

"Welcome!" Thel Dar greeted them.

"Are the enhanced data collectors now sufficiently prepared?" one of them inquired.

"Soon, Kevala. Soon, old friend," Tathata replied.

"Excellent. You will keep us informed?" another asked.

"Of course. It will be done," Thel Dar answered.

In the Land of the Ellipse, the long, splendid night waned. The approaching dawn made the night air feel cold as the stars began to fade in the sky.

Wolfie turned to Gracie, and taking her hand, said, "Let's walk out onto the plateau."

High above the campfire and the ships, Gracie spread out a small blanket on the smooth sandstone. Wolfie looked up into the night sky and then into Gracie's eyes.

"Have you ever wondered why I have not tried to make love to you?" he asked.

Gracie replied, "I don't mind, Wolfie. Our friendship and the closeness we share makes me happy." Gracie had chosen not to be with anyone for some years.

"I myself wondered, but now I understand," Wolfie continued. "And now I want you."

Gracie, startled, smiled.

"When I first borrowed Ed's body, his DNA was severely damaged from alcohol. As time has passed, my transmuting consciousness has healed the genome and activated much of the latent DNA. I have forced the physical brain of Edward Paul Ross to open and adapt to the higher frequencies of my etheric mind. Tonight his DNA is sufficiently altered."

"Sufficiently for what?" Gracie asked innocently.

"To have a baby with you," Wolfie said bluntly.

"Oh, my!" Gracie gasped. "Wolfie, I'm too old, and..."

"Never, my love, never..." Wolfie's reply was to take her in his arms and gently lay her down on the small blanket. Gracie looked up at the sky and saw seven shooting stars fly quickly by, one after the other.

"Did you see that?" she said. Wolfie tenderly kissed her neck as he removed her sweater and jeans. The two lovers lay naked under the fading stars, exposed to the first rays of dawn.

The consciousness of Thel Dar and Tathata was magnetically aligned to the Land of the Ellipse by their three friends, Kevala, Karuna, and Kha.

Kevala hovered near Wolfie and Gracie. "This one is designated for me, is it not?"

Thel Dar beamed like a proud mother. "Yes, Kevala, this one is for you. I know that your dream is to take the music of the spheres to the city named for the angels."

Kevala pondered the future. "Will I be a boy child, or a girl?"

"It is your choice, my friend," Tathata replied. "I trust you to guide Gracie and Wolfie. Of course, Thel Dar and I will be around. Their child will become the appropriate enhanced data-collecting vehicle for you to inhabit. We are very pleased to bring you into our adventure."

"Ah, and such superb DNA to play in," Kevala said. "I am looking forward to this."

Gracie felt every cell in her body heating up, as had happened before on Lost Mountain. But this was different, because Wolfie's energy was involved; and it was sweet because, at long last, they were lovers, and as everyone knows, Prime Creator loves lovers.

The fire that burns but does not consume spread over Gracie. She felt pleasure in every cell. The two lovers tuned their individual rhythms together, uniting them in an undulating motion. Concentric circles of light and sound began to emanate from the lovers, like music, as the purple rays of dawn washed over them. Then the couple became motionless, their hearts and souls suspended in the silence and absolute stillness of that moment. Wolfie entered the fertile darkness of the woman he loved and tenderly spilled his seeds of life.

Gracie thought she glimpsed Thel Dar floating above, with four other figures, in the mist of dawn. Or was there only one mysterious presence spraying silver and golden photons in ever-widening arcs across the high desert. Gracie tried to speak, but could not. Only a faint murmur came from her lips as she fell into an ocean of bliss and all physical awareness disappeared.

Gracie and Wolfie found themselves in the forever Void, surrounded by three magnificent columns of light.

"I am Kevala, dear lady," said a voice from within one of the columns. "I am to have the honor of becoming the child within your womb, with your consent and the cooperation of Herr Mozart. It is my dream to lift the veils from Earth in song."

Gracie and Wolfie looked at Thel Dar and Tathata, and understood. Kevala was to be their child. The winds of change were upon the land, and a new race of beings would follow. Gracie and Wolfie, and all of the human beings who dared to alter their DNA, were to bring the new children into being.

Gracie opened her eyes to the new dawn. Her skin felt the clean cold air and Wolfie reached for their clothes. Pulling on her sweater, Gracie started to cry. Tears of joy ran down her flushed cheeks.

"I was always afraid to have a child, Wolfie," she sobbed.

"I understand," he offered.

"And now it seems that I was only waiting for this moment, and my age doesn't mean a thing. All that matters now is that this being, Kevala, wants to be born through us to help uplift the planet. And that's the most wonderful thing in the world. I've never been so happy."

Wolfie laughed gently and held her close to him.

A baby was coming.

XVI

THE COURAGE TO KNOW

Lord Marduk sneered as the derisive sound that passed for laughter croaked from his throat; he had an idea, a brainstorm. As usual, Marduk's innate genius had prevailed, and he now knew exactly what to do.

Calling his lieutenants to the control room, he grilled them about the renegade aliens who were dealing in smuggled DNA. Informed of the suspect aliens' identities and probable locations, Marduk ordered his gang of trained assassins, the Asuran Special Forces, to bring in the leaders of the renegade smugglers.

"So be it!" they responded.

Within twenty-four hours a mangy bunch of cranky criminal aliens found themselves assembled in one of Marduk's holographic prisons. Large projectors flung the usual scenes of violence, maiming, and overwhelming mayhem against the walls, floor, and ceiling—a ghastly and unnerving sight, really.

"I, Lord Marduk, have long known of your amateur covert activities," Marduk began. "Until now, I did not consider your feeble dealings worthy of my time; but I have found a use for you."

Some of the alien thieves were beginning to tremble; the ominous images projected around them were making them nervous. Most of them were addicted to one chemical substance or another, the effects of which were quickly wearing off in this atmosphere.

"Listen up!" Marduk's red eyes blazed as he noticed his captives' attention drifting. "You will insert yourselves into the time period termed by the Earth humans the 1950s. With my permission and under my aegis, you will be allowed to build genetic experimentation facilities at specific underground locations, where you may carry on any nefarious activities you like."

The raggedy gang perked up at this last pronouncement.

"My protection will cost you eighty percent of your profits. You will accept my terms, or not one of you will ever leave this place. And don't imagine that I intend to relieve you of your corporal existence anytime soon. The displays on the walls will give you a glimpse of your extended future, should you displease me."

Disgruntled moaning spread through the line. "Eighty percent! *Spiffengritz!*"

"Take it or leave it," Marduk demanded, a smile coursing his reptilian lips.

And so the renegade aliens who were dealing in contraband DNA were allowed to build their facilities underneath the Land of the Ellipse, and in other selected geographic locations where Marduk had ascertained that too much energy was being generated for the upliftment of mankind.

For Marduk this was the perfect solution. Now he would balance the scales.

When the aliens inserted themselves into the past, their presence was felt immediately by Anu and the others in the Land of the Ellipse, and the balance of energies clearly shifted.

Anu announced the intrusion. "There has been an alteration in the frequencies of this area. Id, we must return to your people and find a way to counter this."

"It is Marduk," the Commander added. "He must have known we were here, even under the cloaking."

Jehran, skilled in the art of remote viewing, said, "The cloaking device itself would eventually attract his attention. Marduk has traveled back in time and altered history. He has allowed the alien outlaw smugglers to build their sub-terranean bases beneath the surface of the Earth so they may carry out experimental breeding with the human DNA they have stolen."

"Jehran," Inanna said, "let us follow Anu and Id into Inner Earth. I want to see my great-aunt Ninhursag, and there must be something more we can do."

"If that is your wish," Jehran replied.

The party was breaking up. Clarissa and Michael were heading back to the Pacific Northwest. Wolfie wanted to see California; he and Gracie were thinking of driving up the Pacific Coast highway. Jehran and Inanna would follow Anu and Id into Inner Earth. The Lady of the Garnets, the Commander, Antu, and Enlil were leaving for the Mother Ship with the Etherians. All said their farewells.

✳

Thel Dar transferred its focus from the third dimensional reality of the planet Earth. Moving beyond the small blue-green sphere orbiting in its familiar solar system, beyond the Milky Way and its galaxy of stars, Thel Dar withdrew from the dimensions of time and space, and rested in the indigo-blue blackness of the forever Void.

Temporarily satiated with polarities and floating peacefully in the dark silence, Thel Dar contemplated the new possibilities and asked the eternal question: *What next?*

The Earth was certainly exciting, if a little exhausting for its inhabitants. In a free-will Universe, one could never know exactly what might happen; that was precisely what made it so fascinating and attractive. Within the spectrum of third dimensional frequencies, a soul might undergo *anything*.

Thel Dar contemplated all the lives ever lived, those persons loved and lost, the tears shed, the joy and sorrow. Earth provided a holographic stage on which human beings could experience.

The time had come for a further expansion of feeling. Thel Dar and others had successfully developed a new form through which to experience their created realities, an enhanced data-collecting vehicle. The human body was beginning its mutation; within the glittering spirals of deoxyribonucleic acid, the human genome was about to unfold and amplify its realities. Gracie and many like her were ready to play.

The new children were coming to the small blue-green planet to disseminate the frequencies of joy throughout the Universe. A wonderful new adventure was beginning for them all.

In the Twilight of the Kali Yuga, life on Earth was on the precipice of change. Many people were close to realizing just how many layers of realties and dimensional worlds had existed around them all the while. At first this knowledge often came as a shock, but some humans were well prepared for the greater awareness; they would help the others to adjust and to shift their perspective.

The *Living Waters* would flow in the human body once more as individuals came to realize that through the conscious focus of will, they could merge their bodies' fiery primal energies with consciousness to activate the hormonal secretions of the endocrine system—and unlock the rest of the brain.

New synapses would begin to connect and fire, and thus receive new frequencies of information. Previously unnoticed existing realities would begin to open up new adventures for the human species. Boredom would vanish— along with the fear of death, intolerance for others, and the obsession with material wealth. With so many new probabilities available, who would want to dwell in the known past?

Humankind was on the verge of knowing the wonderful truth—that each one alone possessed the power to allow God's embrace. No one had ever needed an intermediary between themselves and God; no one needed to pay money to anyone to remember that they had always been *one* with Prime Creator!

All that was required was an opening of the heart and an invitation to the God within them. No one had ever possessed the power to prevent that Union. No one. Everyone and everything was God veiled. Each one, fueled by eternal and everlasting Love, controlled the veil and the process of remembering. Each was the dreamer and the dream; they had only to *want* it, to remember they *were* it all along!

Thel Dar sighed in the deep darkness of the forever Void. The radiant-light Being smiled, thinking once more of the children, the new children who would be born with the courage to *know* and the capacity to expand their reality without fear.

Inanna slept peacefully beside Jehran in Inner Earth. The meeting with Enki and Ninhursag had been wonderful. Inanna's great-aunt and great-uncle were both thoroughly impressed with Jehran. But the events of the past few days had exhausted the arriving party, and they had been shown to cozy guest rooms to sleep.

In a softly lit room, under silken covers, Inanna slept and dreamed. In the dream she spoke to Spirit.

"My friend, I wander down a darkened corridor. I see a door of glass and wood. My fingers press against the smooth hardness, seemingly solid to my flesh. Knowing the door is my dream within the Dream, I pass through it as a vapor.

"Deep and cold dark waters stretch out before me. Their stillness overwhelms me. In such serenity, moonlight spills out over this ocean. I feel my life slip away, in memory, in ecstasy, in pain. I take with me only the wisdom from the Dream.

"Beyond the door are worlds of chaos, worlds of order. In the place of Love, beyond all shadows, my friends await me. There I meet the Beloved, my soul, my Self. There beyond all Time, we embrace."

The Beloved spoke. "Inanna, I have always loved you. I never judged you. You lost your Self in play, in laughter, and in tears while I waited.

"I followed you down the corridors of Time, waiting for you to turn to me, to remember. To remember the embrace, the sweetness, the purity of our Union. You, lost in the veils of forgetfulness, thought we were separate—and you longed for me.

"Our love has always been, for we are eternally One. I am the Embrace, I am the Beloved, and I am you, my sweet Inanna. I am the Dream and the dreamer veiled within it."

Inanna woke beside Jehran. She opened her eyes and pondered her dream—a dream within the Dream. Lately she felt a recognition of her being a Self beyond Inanna. In one reality she was most definitely her familiar self, Inanna, a loving woman wrapped in a soft blue skin, who once had proclaimed herself the Queen of Heaven on a small blue-green planet. But in a larger reality, Inanna knew herself to be something more.

She loved Jehran; nothing could change that. He was everything she had ever wanted. But within her was another love—one that drew her attention from this reality, as sweet as it was, to another.

Inanna called this compelling force the Beloved, for that is how she experienced it. For Inanna, the Beloved was a love she had always known, yet somehow forgotten. The Beloved was above her, within her, and beneath her. It was her strength, her Source, and the air that she breathed.

Jehran was waking, and Inanna turned to him to look deeply into his eyes. For the first time, she understood that the beauty she had loved in Jehran's brilliant eyes was not Jehran's alone. There, shining from within him, was also the Beloved.

Jehran smiled. He knew what she was feeling and thinking. He always knew.

"I know, my darling," he whispered to her. "I know I am Jehran, and I am something beyond. Free of my apparent being, I am as the morning light and the invisible ocean that holds us. I am you, my Inanna, even as you are me."

"You understand," Inanna said softly, happily.

"Of course. Isn't that the reason you love me?" he asked.

"Yes, I see that now," she replied. "As Jehran and Inanna, we love each other. Yet we are more, and we long for that *more*."

Jehran held her close for a moment. "In the same way that we unite in love, the Beloved within you longs for union with you. It is true for me as well; my soul calls to me. I too am remembering what I have always known."

They both felt a third presence. Inanna spoke.

"It is the child. It waits to be born; it waits for us to remember, to know who we are."

"The child is wonderful."

"We will give it a new home."

"The child waits for us."

"I feel the soul near to us."

"Yes. There is great love."

"Are we ready?" she asked.

"Yes," he replied.

XVII

A FAMILY BREAKFAST

The following morning, Inanna and Jehran sat down
to breakfast with Anu, Id, Ninhursag, and Enki. Anu noticed
a subtle change in Inanna, but decided not to mention it.

Jehran looked around the table at his new family and said
to Enki and Ninhursag, "So, you two are brother and sister?"

Id answered for the siblings. "They have different
mothers. Interesting, isn't it, Jehran? These two bear almost
no resemblance whatsoever, except in the eyes. I've always
thought you both have Anu's eyes." She smiled at them.

Ninhursag flashed a threatening glance at her brother
Enki, warning him not to comment.

"My mother," Ninhursag explained, "lived and worked
on a planet devoted to the arts of healing. She was considered the most brilliant physician and surgeon of her time.

She understood the harm that is done to the body when the spirit within it is not allowed to freely express itself."

Inanna smiled to herself. Ninhursag was proud of her mother and rightly so.

"Id is Enki's mother," Ninhursag continued. "Id's genetic origins are quite unlike those of my mother's people, who came from Altair. The planet of healing was home to a wonderful mixture of races who came together from all across the Universe to work and learn. My traditions and Id's have always been vastly different."

The two women looked at each other. It had taken many years, and Marduk's reign of tyranny, to bring these two intensely self-assured females together.

Anu joined in the conversation concerning his three children. "Enlil's mother is primarily of Pleiadian racial background, as I am. She is my sister and wife, Antu."

Enki spoke to Jehran. "And therein lay the source of our eternal quarrels. Enlil and I could never see eye to eye on anything. He was always so exacting, unbending, and systematic. He never learned to just relax and have fun."

"Now, Enki, don't get started," Ninhursag interrupted. "You are more intuitive and expansive, if somewhat less discriminating in your passions, than Enlil."

"Are you going to start blaming me again for what happened?" Enki asked, turning back to Jehran. "You see, it seems that my son, Marduk, inherited my frustration and anger. Seeing Enlil and I quarrel all our lives, Marduk developed an obsessive determination to seize everything, the entire Earth and beyond, for himself."

The breakfast party suddenly grew silent. Marduk was a sore subject at such family gatherings. Inanna lifted a plate of warm sweet rolls dripping with honeyed raspberries and passed them to Jehran.

"What's done is done," Inanna said. "Our only hope now is to alter the future through our actions in the present. There is nothing to be gained from blaming anyone. We all had a part in creating Marduk."

"Quite correct, my girl!" Anu lifted his glass and made a toast. "Here's to the ever-changing present!"

All joined in the toast, relieved to temporarily set aside the usual family tensions. Inanna changed the subject.

"Ninhursag," she inquired, "tell us what news you have. Is there any further progress to report?"

"There is great fear up on the surface," Ninhursag said sadly. "The children of Earth are anxious and confused, and growing more so as time passes. This date of 2011 that has been given to them only serves to increase their sense of foreboding and worry.

"Marduk continues to pursue his insidious policies. Now he has even allowed groups of renegade aliens to experiment with the human genome in underground laboratories. Stories of these activities have leaked out, greatly exacerbating levels of fear among the earthlings.

"Marduk's continued relentless electronic programming numbs the humans to the voice within them and to the possibilities of activating their own DNA."

Enki interrupted his sister. "However, a growing number of humans are fully immersed in the process of remembering. Because consciousness is contagious, there is an excellent possibility of more awakening to Spirit as each day passes."

Inanna spoke with a gentle pride. "I myself am changing. I just recently have had many extraordinary realizations, and I feel a blessed transformation taking place within me."

Ninhursag reached over and touched Inanna's hand. "How very wonderful! Good for you!" Nin had always loved Inanna; she felt like a mother to her.

"The change must come from within now," Enki reflected. "We can do no more external work with the DNA; we have interfered too much as it is. Now it is up to the humans to individually reconnect the twelve strands of deoxyribonucleic acid, and open the unused portions of their brain to receive an awareness of the rest of the Universe."

"Yes," Id added. "And at last the great Beings, who have patiently waited in the forever Void, can enter these evolved data-collecting vehicles and enjoy a new expression of creation."

"You know about this?" Inanna asked.

"Oh yes, my dear," Id replied. "And I believe I know something about you as well."

Inanna blushed; the family's curiosity was aroused. But Ninhursag tactfully changed the subject and asked about the concert Herr Mozart had given in the Land of the Ellipse; she was very fond of his music. Surely there were other more pressing matters to discuss as well.

Jehran sat quietly observing the family dynamics of Anu and his children. Here was a group of beings whose characters were highly contrasting and intensely individualistic. Jehran realized how necessary it had been for Inanna to become very strong within herself just to survive in such a family. The child now growing within her, Jehran thought, had certainly found some interesting DNA to play in.

XVIII

THE LONELY

Wolfie and Gracie raced down the highway in a rented red sports car. Wolfie had insisted; it had been his dream to ride out into the West in a flashy red convertible. Clarissa and Michael had taken Gracie's truck and the dogs back to the Pacific Northwest. Gracie promised that she and Wolfie would be back home in a week.

First stop—Las Vegas!

"Wolfie, there it is," Gracie exclaimed.

Neither was prepared for the sight of a giant pyramid rising out of the desert amidst neon signs and power lines, but there it was, as big as life.

"Wow! Let's go there first," Wolfie suggested.

The sun was setting as the two pulled off the freeway. As far as their eyes could see, flashing neon lights covered the city. There seemed to be more electric signs than buildings. This endless world of neon lights filled the air with unsettling and bizarre electromagnetic frequencies.

✳

Wolfie pulled into the valet line of the Pyramid Casino Hotel; a young man came out admiring the car's awesome horsepower, and took the keys from them.

"Ya'll enjoy your stay!" he said cheerfully.

"Such a nice young man," Wolfie said to Gracie as they walked through the glittering glass entrance into the giant pyramid.

"Oh, my goodness!" Gracie was amazed. A vague memory crept into her consciousness. She felt herself to be in another time and place, standing beside the real pyramid at Giza in ancient Egypt.

That can't be me, Gracie thought to herself. She was all decked out in a golden warrior's outfit and striking the sides of the stone pyramid with a laser-like sword. Her body was blue, and she was screaming in a strange language that she did not comprehend. Gracie suspected the language was not at all nice; in fact, she was sure it was obscene.

"This must be one of Inanna's memories," Gracie said out loud.

"What? No, we're actually here. This is not a memory, is it?" Wolfie asked.

"Never mind. Let's walk around." Gracie led Wolfie down into the casinos.

Wolfie was amazed. "I've never seen anything like this! I often gambled in Austria, but nothing even remotely like this existed then."

At first Wolfie was really excited by all the lights and

noise. There were hundreds of games all lit up, and crowds of people sitting and standing around tables, machines, and bars. Wolfie wanted to play.

But then, "Gracie, look at that!" he said.

Above them were shadows hovering over the gamblers. Dark black vapors shape-shifted over and around every person on the casino floor.

"What *is* that?" Gracie asked.

"Phantoms," Wolfie answered. "Look, they get larger and smaller."

He pointed to a wild-haired woman who was obviously losing the last of her money. The woman became more and more distraught as she downed her drink and dropped the last of her quarters into the greedy box with its flashing lights.

Gracie and Wolfie glanced around them. Everywhere they looked they saw emptiness. It was as if these people hoped to fill up their lonely lives with noise and flashing lights, with the hope that one day Lady Luck would smile on them.

"Come on, Wolfie. Let's get out of here. Let's go to the club with the rock and roll museum, okay?"

"Okay." Wolfie put his arm around Gracie and the two headed for the exit.

Wolfie fantasized about what it would be like to be a rock star with millions of adoring female fans and groupies, with computerized laser-light shows and the new electronic instruments, like synthesizers. Music in his time had been very different, and Wolfie happily imagined himself as a twentieth-century rock and roll phenomenon.

He and Gracie entered the casino/museum. Enormous glass cases displayed the fabulous sequined costumes once worn by famous rock stars. Wolfie paused before each glittering suit, picturing how he might have looked in such attire.

"Music is big business these days, Wolfie," Gracie said.

Wolfie understood. "In my time, the king was big business."

Gracie laughed, thinking that in a museum of rock and roll, the "king" could only be Elvis.

Wolfie looked up; quadraphonic speakers blasted rock and roll tunes out across the casino below them; saxophones and electric guitars hung from the ceiling. In the center was a piano covered with rhinestones.

"Oh my, that is gaudy! This is fun," Wolfie said. "But something is missing, don't you feel?"

"You mean it's not really a place for music?"

"It's a place for gambling. Let's go," Wolfie said. "I had enough of gambling in my last life."

Back in the car, driving down the freeway in the night, Gracie put on some old rock and roll and turned the volume up high as the two headed for Beverly Hills and the Pacific Ocean.

Beyond the ionosphere, Marduk was sound asleep, orbiting planet Earth in his private ship. He was loudly snoring a reptilian snore, but the harsh noises coming from his perfect nose had no effect on his deep repose. Marduk was dreaming.

In his dream, he was a young man again, living in ancient Egypt before he had taken Earth from Enlil—before Marduk had come into his own power. He was in a room with his father, Enki, and his aunt, Ninhursag; as usual, they were beginning to really annoy him. It was not at all clear to Marduk exactly what he had done in the dream to make them so bothersome; but by the nanosecond, Marduk was becoming more and more angered.

If Enki had been the only one present, Marduk could have easily overwhelmed him and put an end to the discussion. His father was a pushover, a weak and spineless excuse for a man who was easily manipulated. There were times when Marduk was sure that Enki was actually afraid of his own son.

But that willful female Ninhursag was hovering over Enki, pressuring him to stand firm. Marduk knew that Enki would oppose him simply to look good in his sister's eyes. Enki would have to make a show of standing up to his son.

That shrew of a woman was going on and on about— what was she saying?

"What's your point, Ninhursag?" Marduk interrupted her rudely.

Nin laughed at him derisively. "Listen to me, my little spoiled self-centered nephew. Don't you take that tone with me. I've known you all your life, and I'm well acquainted with your nature. Unlike your father here, I have no fear of you."

Enki protested, "I am not afraid of him!"

At that both Ninhursag and Marduk smirked.

"Well, whatever," Nin continued. "But I can promise you this, young man…"

At this point the dream began to shift and distort. Ninhursag's words became giant geometric clouds: Maxims such as "…know you are a part of creation" and "…one with your Source" floated toward Marduk's head. He ducked.

Enki and Ninhursag faded, enfolded by a vaporous mist. Nin's last words hung in the air.

"Someday you'll be all alone, and you'll be very bored, and very weary."

Marduk woke from his dream with a gasp; he was sweating heavily. He had always disliked that damnable female. She was so condescending, even worse than Inanna in some ways. The fact that Ninhursag was Anu's only legitimate daughter made her a formidable and irksome opponent, a real thorn in his side.

What the hell did she mean by that anyway—alone and bored? Marduk thought how he now owned practically everything, and could amuse himself with almost anything he wanted. So how could he, of all people, be bored? He possessed hordes of clones to wait on him hand and foot, not to mention the sniveling human lackeys who slavishly followed his commands in the hope of gaining power for themselves.

Marduk sighed and got up to get himself a glass of water.

Truly, the Kali Yuga wasn't as much fun as it used to be, and he had no idea why. For a moment he felt empty and confused; why did owning everything in it make the world uninteresting? He still enjoyed controlling and dominating everything and everyone; but even that was beginning to get old. Everything was so predictable.

He looked in the mirror. "Get a grip on yourself, old man. Are you losing your edge?" He set down the empty glass and checked his wickedly handsome face for skin tightness; he despised sagging *anything*.

Marduk blinked his red eyes; in the mirror, he saw a

light beside him. He turned quickly, but it was gone. Looking back in the mirror, he saw it again. The light grew, and he heard a familiar, unwelcome voice.

"Marduk, are you done? Ready to come home? Have you finished playing at this game?"

Deep within Marduk's soul, he heard a loud cracking noise, and for a brief moment he remembered something, an emotion, a place—a memory was emerging, the feeling of which he had not known in a very long time.

Immediately this memory became so painful that he shut it down at once. His body bent over in anguish as he screamed aloud.

"No...*no!*"

He fell to the floor, overwhelmed in remembering, he fought back hot tears.

His servants rushed in to assist their master. But Marduk only shrieked at them.

"Get the hell out, you fools!"

And so they left him there on the floor in front of the mirror—all alone.

XIX

HUNGER

Olnwynn had followed Gracie and Wolfie to Las Vegas to keep an eye on them. Talk of the pyramid had seduced him, and he really wanted to see Las Vegas.

Brent and Diana also tagged along for the fun; they and Olnwynn were practically inseparable these days. They had a lot to talk about. After all, Gracie was Brent and Diana's daughter.

Hovering near the ceiling in the great modern pyramid, the three friends were confused by the dazzling lights and ringing machines below them. Olnwynn was looking at the strange synthetic rocks on the walls and trying to locate Gracie when he realized that Diana and Brent were fighting. The two were in the midst of a ridiculous and heated argument about where one could get the best chilies rellenos. Olnwynn was bewildered.

"What's that?" he asked.

"You never ate chilies rellenos?" Brent asked in disbelief.

"No, I didn't," said Olnwynn. He felt left out.

"It was Brent's favorite Mexican dish. He just loved it," Diana said. "That's probably what gave him his heart attack."

"Oh no, that was your fried chicken," Brent corrected her. "You made the best fried chicken in the state."

Olnwynn was getting depressed. He had never tasted a chicken that had been fried, and he didn't have the least idea what this rail-yanos thing was. All this talk was making the three of them yearn to taste food once again. There were definite advantages to being in a body that enjoyed the sense of taste. They gazed down longingly at one of the restaurants near the casino.

"There's sure a lot of places to eat here," Brent said wistfully.

"Let's just go look," Diana suggested.

The three were immediately magnetized to the dessert table. Floating above the double-fudge chocolate cake, the lemon meringue pie, and the strawberry tarts was beginning to make them a little crazy.

Then they noticed they weren't alone. In addition to the living humans still walking around in flesh-and-blood bodies, there were plenty of other life forms—some not so attractive.

"Yikes!" Diana said. "What is that?"

A dark blob of a thing was somehow managing to suck the life energy right out of a big coconut cream pie.

"Yuck! That's disgusting," Brent exclaimed.

"Hmmm, I think we have a lot to learn about the so-called after-life." Olnwynn glanced around him and saw a variety of unusual energy forms.

"They seem to be ignoring us," Brent said.

Olnwynn took that as a challenge and floated over to one particularly nasty-looking phantom.

"Who are you?" he said bravely to the dark ooze.

"Not that it's any of your business, but if you must know, I'm a collection of thought forms put off by humans. I'm a frequency known as anxiety, of the subvariety which produces gluttony. Now go away and leave me alone; I'm waiting for my dinner."

"Zounds!" Olnwynn was temporarily spooked, and the three hastily floated out of the dining area.

They wanted to see the main gambling area; but there the air was thick with dark shadowy phantoms darting above the crowds of unsuspecting people.

"Let's get out of here!" Diana urged.

"Anyone for the Grand Canyon?" Brent genially inquired, forgetting all about Gracie and Wolfie.

"Excellent idea," Olnwynn answered. "And then I'm headed north to check on Gracie's wolves."

Diana laughed. "They're dogs, Olnwynn, not wolves."

With that, the three friends popped right out of the capstone of the great fake pyramid and headed for Arizona.

Gracie and Wolfie pulled into the hotel entrance in their red convertible. Wolfie was amazed by Los Angeles; he had never seen anything like it, and was eager to explore the entire city. But Gracie had other ideas.

The hotel was surrounded by beautiful gardens with roses, bougainvillea, and hibiscus flowering everywhere. A bellboy showed them to their room, and Gracie handed the uniformed young man some money as he recited a list of the hotel's amenities.

"Where is the pool?" Gracie asked.

Wolfie was scrutinizing the young man's uniform, wondering what army he belonged to.

"I can show you the pool, if you like," the friendly fellow replied.

Following him down a lovely winding stone path through lush gardens, Gracie and Wolfie passed through a large iron gate and came upon an oval turquoise swimming pool surrounded by white lounge chairs. Beautiful women in small bathing suits were lounging on the poolside chairs, accompanied by men of every description.

Wolfie was beside himself with childlike curiosity.

"Gracie," he asked, "Why do these people knowingly sit out in the sun and bake themselves? In my time the women went to great lengths to keep their skin as pale as ivory. I do like their costumes."

Gracie just laughed and pointed Wolfie toward a table laid out with fruits, breads, and cheeses. After Wolfie filled up his plate, the two sat down by the pool and Gracie ordered two glasses of cold white wine.

"Let's just relax!" she said pleasantly.

Wolfie decided to humor her for the moment, and lay down beside her to enjoy his plate of peaches, croissant, and double-cream Brie. The pool and the surrounding gardens were intoxicating; it was fun to observe the people.

The two lovers were halfway through their glasses of wine when a woman walking by seemed suddenly to recognize Gracie and headed toward them.

"Gracie! Is that you? My gawd! I haven't seen you for years. We thought you fell off the face of the earth being up there in that New York City for so many years!"

Gracie squinted. Was it really Charlotte Sue Ellen Barrington?

"Charlotte Sue Ellen?" she asked timidly.

"In the flesh, Honey. My, my, who is this young gentleman sittin' here with you?"

Gracie introduced Wolfie, and Charlotte Sue Ellen quickly turned all of her considerable attentions to the man.

"My, you should have a swim, Mr. Wolfie. Is that really your name?"

Wolfie stood up, and, noticing her gold bracelets, perfectly lacquered red nails, and extravagantly large diamond ring, kissed her hand.

Charlotte Sue Ellen Barrington had attended finishing school with Gracie; she came from one of the oldest and wealthiest families in Gracie's hometown. Charlotte Sue Ellen had a passion for the social hierarchy she had been born to rule, and very little interest in anything else.

Gracie smiled gently at her old classmate and tried to remember. She thought about how different life had been then and how much she, Gracie, had changed over the years. She looked into Charlotte Sue Ellen's eyes and saw her soul's light shining from somewhere in there under the false smiles and makeup. Gracie knew that happiness was an elusive commodity, even for the very rich. Charlotte Sue Ellen's armor of perfection could not conceal her desperation.

Charlotte Sue Ellen returned Gracie's smile as she recited the histories of all the people the two women had ever known in common. Gracie was amazed by how much information Charlotte Sue Ellen had managed to retain about so many people—their marriages, their children, their divorces, sometimes their deaths.

Charlotte Sue Ellen soon realized there wasn't anything more to say. After an awkward silence, Gracie stood up and hugged her old acquaintance.

"Well, it was nice seeing you, Honey. I'll tell everyone back home I ran into you."

"Good-bye," Gracie said. "I wish you happiness."

As she walked away, Charlotte Sue Ellen thought, *What an odd thing to say*. But then, Gracie had always been a little strange; she just never could fit in. She always had to be different. Getting her appointment book out of her handbag, Charlotte Sue Ellen Barrington decided not to give it a second thought. Tonight she was invited to a big gala affair.

Gracie turned to Wolfie, who was busy assembling his third plate of snacks.

"Wolfie, have you ever wondered about your identity? I mean, who are you? For that matter, who are any of us?"

Wolfie's mouth was full, so Gracie carried on alone.

"We all think we are an identity, someone we recognize when we look in the mirror or sign our name. But then we meet someone we knew a long time ago; they still see us the way we were at the time they knew us, and they treat us as if we are exactly the same person they knew then. We usually even try to accommodate them by attempting to retrieve old memories and behavior patterns; but the strain is predictably too great, and we all move on."

Wolfie swallowed. "I think I understand. Sometimes I wonder who I am, especially being in Ed Ross's body. I can access the data stored in his cellular memory and I clearly know that those are his experiences, separate from mine.

But as time passes, I absorb the things he learned and so somehow I am him as well as myself, Wolfgang Amadeus Mozart."

"Maybe," Gracie proposed, "we are never really *any* fixed identity. Maybe we are all unique sets of data, accumulations of changing amounts of information, that we falsely perceive to be our identity."

"And," Wolfie added, "perhaps as we merge with other accumulations of data, we expand ourselves and thus our perceived identity. Perhaps all we ever are is our capacity to receive data."

"Yes," Gracie agreed. "As information gatherers for Prime Creator, who we are at any given moment depends on our capacity to receive input. If you never had an identity to begin with, you could never lose it."

At that, the sun and the wine began to make them feel sleepy, and Gracie and Wolfie dozed off beside the turquoise waters of a hotel pool in Beverly Hills.

XX

SNOWLIGHT

Clarissa sat at her window at home, waiting for an unseasonable snowstorm. Weather reports had warned of a possible six inches of the white stuff.

Clarissa had put out an assortment of wild seeds for the juncos and finches to sustain them through the impending storm. She was one of those women born with all of her nurturing instincts intact; babies, birds, and strays could count on her loving care. She kept a protective eye out for the neighborhood cats, who might like to pounce upon the unsuspecting birds.

Dreaming of Michael's baby, Clarissa put her hand on her womb to feel for signs. So far she felt no change, no swelling, no nausea, and no craving for the proverbial pickles and ice cream.

Michael walked into the room and sat beside her. In silence the lovers looked out at the winter sky, the evergreens, and the chickadees. Big wet snowflakes began to fall. The temperature was just barely freezing, and the snowflakes looked like crystal fairy dancers. The pristine beauty of the scene transfixed Clarissa and Michael; each unique snowflake was part of an intricate, elegant ballet.

"I love you," Michael said softly as he turned to embrace Clarissa.

They looked into each other's eyes; the light they saw there drew them into another world. A powerful energy began to flow between them, and they could no longer feel where one ended and the other began. The walls and windows around them disappeared; the falling snow formed a spiraling vortex which encircled the couple with dancing crystals.

Clarissa and Michael felt themselves becoming lighter and lighter. As the snow which burned like starlight carried them up into the spiral, they could hear the birds singing. Somewhere in the heavens, a single cello played a hauntingly familiar melody.

Engulfed in this whirling spiral of light, Michael and Clarissa began to make love with their minds. Instinctively they knew there was no need to touch. Their thoughts were more powerful than any of the five senses.

The *Living Waters* began to flow in and through the couple. Primary energy moved up their bodies as fire and interchanged with their consciousness as water. Because the *Living Waters* flowed from one to the other and back again, energy was amplified. Concurrently, the lovers' consciousness was vivified, endowed with Life, and tempered by Spirit. The experience of the *Living Waters* allowed the Spirit within Michael and Clarissa to expand itself in and through them.

The spiral of light which held the lovers, and the flow-ing exchange of fire, attracted Thel Dar, Tathata, and their friends—along with the Watchers, whose job it is to observe the progress of creation.

As the beauty of the spiraling vortex increased in intensity, layers of simple melodies spread throughout the Universe, echoing the sweet songs of the small birds in Clarissa's garden.

Thel Dar turned to Karuna and spoke.

"Well, my friend, the time has come for you to enter the enhanced data collector we have labored so intently to create for you. Are you ready?"

Karuna smiled at Thel Dar and Tathata. "Dear friends, what an adventure you have provided for me! I will endeavor to bring a pure compassion to Earth. The joy of my ensuing experiences shall be shared by all. My heart is with you. Farewell, and thanks be to you."

Tathata spoke one last word of warning.

"You are aware, Karuna, that none of us knows exactly what will happen. We can only set up certain probabilities and proclivities based on the structural integrity of the genome. No one ever knows how things will turn out."

"Ah, yes," Karuna replied. "I have been warned. But is that not what makes a free-will Universe so exciting? Do not be concerned; I will remember."

"Yes!" Thel Dar added. "You be sure to remember! Fare thee well, old friend."

At last Michael and Clarissa embraced within the spiral; the union of their physical bodies spilled out as powerful harmonies within all-the-possible worlds. In that moment, Karuna entered the vortex of spinning, spiraling,

phosphorescent photons that was Michael and Clarissa—
and lost itself in Bliss.

Back in their bed in the small house in the Pacific
Northwest on planet Earth, Michael held Clarissa in his
arms. He drifted into a deep sleep while Clarissa, snuggled
into his warm body, listened intently to the white silence of
the snow outside.

There was nothing to think about, not a single
worry—only the warmth of Michael's skin next to hers, the
rich dark shadows that moved across their house, and the
silence of a winter's night. Clarissa smiled the smile that
mothers know as she felt the child taking form within her.

XXI

FRIENDS

It was late evening in Inner Earth. Inanna sat in Ninhursag's dressing rooms. The two women shared a closeness based on their family ties; Ninhursag had taken care of Inanna as a small child on Nibiru.

In the early days of Earth's colonization, there were frequent and unpredictable radiation storms. Inanna's mother had shipped Inanna and her twin brother off to the home planet Nibiru to protect the children's invaluable DNA. Inanna had been placed in Ninhursag's loving, if somewhat rigorous, care. Such bonds last for life and require little renewal.

Inanna and Ninhursag talked deep into the night; even though it was late, neither felt tired. The room was bathed in a soft light and the two women spoke quietly.

There was much to share; they loved each other and their stories energized them.

"Nini, how you have changed." Ninhursag addressed Inanna by the childhood nickname she had called her on Nibiru. Nini meant "little girl," and when Ninhursag used the word, the word was uniquely imbued with love.

No two women could have been more profoundly different; in many ways, they were exact opposites. Yet an enduring affection based on mutual respect flowed between them. During the course of their lives, they had frequently teased each other, occasionally quarreled, at times even stopped speaking. But their love had remained; the bond was unbroken.

Throughout the years on planet Earth no man had been Ninhursag's equal. Except for her two brothers, Enlil and Enki, who were themselves married, no one was ideally suited for the daughter of Anu. Consequently, she had retreated into herself and her work at the hospital. A formidable intellect, combined with her skills as a physician and genetic scientist, had further isolated this elegant and beautiful woman.

Almost everyone was intimidated by Ninhursag, except Inanna. Because of the bond between them, Inanna was invariably able to draw out her great-aunt with a little humor and a lot of love.

Inanna was sure that Ninhursag needed only to be dragged back into life. Inanna knew Ninhursag shared her own passion for life and the living. Remembering the great love and tenderness Ninhursag had shown her as a child, Inanna had resolved to relentlessly pursue the awesome task of dragging her beloved great-aunt Nin out of her protective shell.

For the most part, the only person with whom Ninhursag could relax and be herself was Inanna. Tonight Ninhursag was filled with praise for her little Nini.

"Nini, I am proud of you. The disposition of your character has emerged all the better, my girl. Your love for the people of Earth and your fearless entry into their body-vehicles have given you wisdom. You are now a woman who possesses a grandly expanded consciousness, and the depth of your feelings has contributed to the beauty of your soul."

"Oh, Nin!" Inanna answered. "At last I have truly pleased you. There appears to be progress on the Earth. Many are waking up and remembering the Spirit within them. Many are traveling in their consciousness from one layer of dimensional reality to another. This is an exciting time to be alive.

"When the humans realize that they can access other dimensional realities, they will become accustomed to seeing us and will not fear us. When that time comes, I want to live once again on the planet's surface. Jehran and I have a plan to build a wonderful home in the Himalayan foothills. We want to raise our children there, and we want you to come with us."

Inanna tried to stifle her excitement, but her eyes twinkled, making Ninhursag simultaneously suspicious and amused.

"All right, young lady, what scheme are you up to? You have some wild idea in that non-linear mind of yours, I can clearly see."

"Oh, not really anything clearly in mind," Inanna protested. "There will be much healing work to do, and Jehran has this friend that he and I think you might enjoy meeting."

Ninhursag laughed out loud. Only Inanna would dare

to fix up the daughter of Anu with a date; only Inanna would have the nerve even to suggest such a match.

"Inanna, you know very well that I have not even so much as looked at a man in many years."

"I know," Inanna replied sweetly. "But you are still beautiful, with so much love yet to give."

At that Ninhursag was silent. She reflected on all the years she had spent in research and the practice of healing. She thought of her frayed relationships with her two brothers, Enki and Enlil. Time had indeed passed. Her life had been full and rich with experience; and yet, conceivably, now was the time for change. Perhaps she was ready for a new adventure. The thought of living near the great Himalayan mountains captured her imagination. Inanna was clever, after all.

"Well, we shall see."

"At least you will consider my offer?" Inanna persisted, as stubborn as always. "Jehran wants you to come."

"Yes, I will consider it." Ninhursag said. "But now I want to draw a sample of your blood to study what you have done to your DNA with all this expanded consciousness you have achieved."

"Tonight?" Inanna was not interested. "Oh no, Nin. Yuck! Tomorrow I will come to the laboratory. There you and Enki can stick needles into me to your hearts' content. But tonight I'm going to my bed to dream of a new home in the mountains where my children can play."

Inanna kissed Nin goodnight.

"I love you too." Ninhursag sighed. There was so much between them, so much these two opposites understood and knew about each other.

"Good night, my Nin."

"Good night, little Nini. Sweet dreams."

XXII

THE CALL

Everyone was sound asleep. Ninhursag, Enki, and Id, along with Inanna and Jehran, slept peacefully deep within Inner Earth. Wolfie and Gracie were in Beverly Hills, Clarissa and Michael in the Pacific Northwest. Anu and Antu were on the Mother Ship with their son Enlil, and with the Commander and the Lady of the Garnets.

In their dreams came *The Call*. It came as a resonating tone which drew them into an awareness. Each receiver knew and understood, for the call was elemental.

In the Eye of the Mind, the holographic image of an ancient primordial valley presented itself. Monolithic stones filled the valley and cast purple shadows over the desolate land. This place was a central point, a convergence of consciousness, and a familiar home.

All of the dreamers focused their consciousness intently into the valley of monolithic stones, and with a single purpose of mind projected themselves, as thought, to that place. Olnwynn, Diana, and Brent had also received the call and had come there together.

In silence, the group formed a circle. They were pleased to see one another, pleased to be together again. A light appeared above them and showered photons all around them. The photons metamorphosed into Thel Dar, Tathata, and other radiant-light Beings, who then surrounded the circle of friends with a dome of golden light.

As they all stood there bathing in radiance, the Lady of the Garnets purposefully left the circle and walked over to one of the massive rocks scattered across this primeval valley. Turning back toward the others, smiling, she beckoned to them to join her as she moved right through what had appeared to be an impenetrable wall of granite. One by one, each of the others followed her.

Inside the granite wall was an enormous oval room made of solid rock with no visible entrances or exits. Once more the members of the small group formed a circle and began to focus their awareness. The granite walls glistened with quartz crystal as the tone that had first called them became a timeless ancient song, and together they began to sing.

Sound waves imbued the stone walls with pulsating harmonic vibrations. Thel Dar and the other radiant-light Beings floated above the circle, emitting knowledge as light.

Everyone in the oval emitted his or her individual energy as light and sound; each unique emanation blended with every other to create a wonderful interplay of knowledge and beauty. It was a divine marriage of sorts, among these who were bonded by blood and by soul.

The energy generated by the fusing of these friends raised the frequency of the granite stone oval. In the ceiling above them appeared a geometric array of large multicolored crystals.

"This is a matrix for healing," Thel Dar said softly.

Beneath the outcrop of crystals, a table of lapis lazuli and gold appeared.

"Yes, I understand," Ninhursag said. "Here we may heal the DNA of those who make the choice to become multidimensional."

Thel Dar smiled. "The love you bear, all of you, for life on Earth has brought forth this dream of healing."

Twelve doors then appeared in the circle of rock surrounding them. Each door was splendidly unique; some were covered with golden carvings and jewels, while others were simply carved of rough strong wood. Others were transparent and led into endless tunnels of light.

"These doors represent openings to possible dimensional realities, nested one within the other," Thel Dar told them. "As the human mind begins to open and expand itself, you may bring individuals to this place, in the dream state or in meditation, so that they may become aware of all-the-possible worlds. Once they learn to access new and ever expanding realities for themselves, they will no longer need to come here. Until such time, this place will be here to serve them."

"By the power of your love, you have created this place in your consciousness," Tathata explained. "In the spirit of adventure and fun, this opening is intended to further the evolution of the human species. Use it wisely."

The radiant-light Beings disappeared, and the little group found itself alone within the granite walls. The Commander, Olnwynn, and Michael immediately began to explore the doors; just touching the doors gave them a surge of a particular frequency.

"This is going to be fun!" Michael exclaimed.

Ninhursag was watching Michael and admiring his courage when she noticed Inanna. The older woman looked intently at Inanna and, in that moment, somehow sensed a profoundly new change in her. The Lady of the Garnets felt Ninhursag's astonishment, and, seeing the transformation for herself, walked toward Inanna to embrace her dear friend in happiness.

Inanna, suddenly distracted by what she saw in Gracie and Clarissa, didn't notice Ninhursag or the Lady of the Garnets and began walking toward the young women. As they all came together near the lapis table, the women at once realized that something wonderful had happened. The women began to cry, and the men turned around to see what was up.

Everyone was crying—Id and Antu, Ninhursag and the Lady of the Garnets. Instinctively they knew that a marvelous wonder had taken place within these three women. Life was evolving. The playing field of Prime Creator had been lifted to a new plateau.

Inanna's eyes sparkled as she offered her hands to Gracie and Clarissa, and in unison, the three said—

"You too?"

"Yes, yes."

"I'm having…"

"Yes!"

"So am I."

"Yes."

"…a child!"

Sleeping peacefully within the womb of each woman lay the promise of hope and the future of this Earth.

Friendly companions to *Inanna Hyper-Luminal*:

Close Extraterrestrial Encounters, Positive Experiences with Mysterious Visitors, Richard J. Boylan and Lee K. Boylan; Wild Flower Press, 1994.

The Mahabharata, translated and edited by J.A.B. van Buitenen; University of Chicago Press, 1973.

Books by Alain Danielou:

  The Gods of India: Hindu Polytheism; Inner Traditions International Ltd, 1985.

  While the Gods Play: Shaiva Oracles and Predictions on the Cycles of History and the Destiny of Mankind; Inner Traditions International Ltd, 1985.

  Virtue, Success, Pleasure, & Liberation: The Four Aims of Life in the Tradition of Ancient India; Inner Traditions International Ltd, 1993.

Books by Julius Evola:

  Revolt Against the Modern World; Inner Traditions International Ltd, 1995.

  The Yoga of Power: Tantra, Shakti, and the Secret Way; Inner Traditions International Ltd, 1992.

Testimony of Light, by Helen Greaves; Neville Spearman Publishers, Essex England, 1993.

Quantum Reality: Beyond the New Physics, by Nick Herbert; Anchor Press / Doubleday, 1985.

Hua Hu Ching, The Later Teachings of Lao Tzu, translated and written by Hua-Ching Ni; Shambala, 1995.

Books by Doris Lessing:

Briefing for a Descent into Hell, 1971.

Canopus in Argos: Archives; Vintage International, 1992.

Books by Barbara Marciniak:

Bringers of the Dawn; Bear and Co., 1992.

Earth; Bear and Co., 1995.

Books by Zecharia Sitchin:

The 12th Planet, 1976.

The Stairway to Heaven, 1980.

The Wars of Gods and Men, 1985.

Divine Encounters, A Guide to Visions, Angels, and Other Emissaries, 1995.

(all Avon bookss)

For extra copies of *Inanna Hyper-Luminal*, send a check or money order in the amount of $14.00 (which includes shipping and handling) to:

Thel Dar Publishing Co.
10002 Aurora Ave. N., #3392
Seattle, Washington 98133-9334